BAUDELAIRE, SARTRE AND CAMUS

BAUDELAIRE, SARTRE AND CAMUS

LECTURES AND COMMENTARIES

GARNET REES, M.A. (Wales)
Docteur de l'Université de Paris

Professor of Modern French Literature
in the University of Hull

UNIVERSITY OF WALES PRESS
CARDIFF
1976

© University of Wales Press, 1976
ISBN 0 7083 0601 2

Printed in Wales by
CSP PRINTING LTD., ST. FAGAN'S ROAD
FAIRWATER, CARDIFF

Contents

Foreword

THE present age is witness to much debate on the theory and practice of education, on its fundamental aims and purposes and the resources which should be devoted to it. Whatever avenues are explored, we should never lose sight of the salient fact that the quality of any system of education, any school or college, however elaborately equipped, is only as good as the quality of its teachers. Engrossed as they are in the daily practice of their vocation, they need the opportunity to survey their work, to discuss their professional problems with colleagues from other schools and colleges in other parts of the country and, perhaps above all, to refresh themselves by a renewed contact in depth with the subject discipline in which they have been trained. Knowledge does not stand still; the teacher has the right to be given the opportunity to test his ideas and to renew himself in the company of colleagues who are specialists in the particular field.

The lectures and commentaries in this book were given on such an occasion, a course entitled *The Sixth-form study of Literature in Modern Languages* held under the auspices of the Department of Education and Science and Her Majesty's Inspectorate in Wales, in Bangor in September 1971, repeated in March 1972. These lectures and the discussions which ensued are a profession of faith that literature should be a catalysing agent in the education of the young. They are a defence and illustration of the words of Albert Camus, taken from his *Discours de Suède* pronounced on 10 December 1957 when he received the Nobel Prize for Literature:

Je ne puis vivre personnellement sans mon art. Mais je n'ai jamais placé cet art au-dessus de tout. S'il m'est nécessaire au contraire, c'est qu'il ne se sépare de personne et me permet de vivre, tel que je suis, au niveau de tous. L'art n'est pas à mes yeux une réjouissance solitaire. Il est un moyen d'émouvoir le plus grand nombre d'hommes en leur offrant une image privilégiée des souffrances et des joies communes. Il oblige donc l'artiste à ne pas s'isoler; il le soumet à la vérité la plus humble et la plus universelle.

ERYL O. DAVIES, H.M.I.,
Chief Inspector, Wales

Introduction

THE origin of these lectures and commentaries is to be found in a course entitled 'The Sixth Form Study of Literature in Modern Languages' held in the University College of North Wales, Bangor, in September 1971 and repeated in March 1972, under the auspices of the Department of Education and Science and Her Majesty's Inspectors of Schools (Modern Languages) in Wales. The course reflected a commonly-held belief in the value of the interchange of ideas between teachers and lecturers in Further and Higher Education, the Inspectorate and University teachers; in the importance of 'post-graduate' refresher courses for graduates who may have left their Universities some time ago; in the discussion and practice in 'workshops' of literary commentary as a means of teaching. Much friendly talk was engendered and it seemed amply demonstrated that the aims of the course had been achieved. It was flatteringly suggested that some of the lectures and commentaries I had given should be published in the hope that they would be useful to sixth formers and undergraduates. They appear here largely as they were given with the minimum of stylistic adjustment to make the spoken word more agreeable when read.

Of all the pedagogic methods used in the teaching of French, the method of *explication de texte* is the only one we have imported wholesale from France. So closely is it identified with the country of its origin that it is known as *l'explication française* and indeed this is the title of a famous manual by G. Rudler, Professor of French at the University of Oxford until the years after the second World War. The method seems to have been introduced into England in the twenties; in France it had long been an instrument of *l'enseignement secondaire. L'explication de texte* has an ancient and distinguished history; throughout the Middle Ages and down to our time, the art of understanding and interpreting texts is still the staple training of theologians, although now known as exegesis, gloss or commentary. It is still essential in the study of Law. To this tradition we must add the study of rhetoric with its analysis of *inventio* (what to say), *dispositio* (in what order to say it) and *elocutio* (how to say it). French literature has a strong tradition of support for these pedagogic ideals. The aims of the Pléiade group of poets, centred around Ronsard and Du Bellay, accept the principle of creative imitation and the values of models chosen among the great writers of antiquity. The seventeenth century saw

1

the development of 'rules' like *bienséance* and *vraisemblance* which were accepted by writer, critic and reader alike. These traditions were passed into the educational system founded by Napoleon under the influence of Jesuit theories of education. This is the background of critics like Lanson, Mornet and Rudler, arch-priests of the method; it is a background which is very different from what happened in England.

It is against this rigid and over-stylized method of *explication de texte* that influential voices have been raised. The late Professor P. Mansell Jones elegantly dismembered it in a paper called 'The Formal Method Arraigned' (in *The Assault* on *French Literature*, Manchester University Press, 1963), following the example of Professor Eugène Vinaver's brilliant presidential address to the Modern Languages Association, given in 1961 ('Le Chêne et le roseau', *Modern Languages*, XLII, 1, March, 1961). I shall try to summarize their objections.

Professor Vinaver quotes a sentence from one of the most famous manuals, M. Roustan's *Précis d'Explication française*, 1911: 'Nous faisons pour décomposer le texte ce que l'auteur a fait pour le composer'. Vinaver goes on, with indignation in every syllable: 'The statement presupposes that we *know* what the author did and how the text was composed, and lest there be any uncertainty or hesitation the manual tells exactly how the author's—*any* author's mind works: "Il est parti d'un fait dominant, d'une idée maîtresse, d'un sentiment qu'il a voulu traduire et nous faire partager . . . Il l'a suivi dans son développement normal, régulier, continu, d'étape en étape"'. The whole thing falls into three main stages, continues Professor Vinaver quoting: "Il y a trois temps dans toute composition littéraire: l'esprit cherche les thèmes ou les arguments qu'il va développer, —il les place dans l'ordre le plus favorable,—il les traduit aussi exactement et artistiquement qu'il le peut". Vinaver remarks that this goes back to the old rhetorical progression of *inventio, dispositio, elocutio.* One must agree entirely with these strictures. Written in 1911, Roustan's analyses do not deal with the real processes of literary creation; he presents the writer as though all writers were alike, as though all literature is concerned with logical argument. But Paul Valéry, that most challengingly lucid of writers, devoted the poems of *Charmes* to an examination of the mysteries of literary creation and confessed that the first idea of *Le Cimetière marin* came to him, not as thought, but in the form of a wordless, obsessional rhythm of the decasyllabic line. Many of the surrealist poets sought to compose by automatic writing, thus denying the rôle of logical reasoning.

Secondly, the insistence upon the analysis of literature as though it were always expository falsifies the understanding of poetry, especially post-Baudelairean poetry. Professor Mansell Jones reminds us of the famous story of the encounter between Mallarmé and Degas. Degas, the painter, was interested in the practice of poetry and once said to Mallarmé: 'J'ai beaucoup de difficultés avec mes sonnets. Je suis plein d'idées mais les mots ne viennent pas'. To this Mallarmé replied: 'Mon cher Degas, la poésie se fait, non pas avec les idées, mais avec les mots'. There is a paradox here: even if a literature of suggestion escapes dogmatic methods of analysis, nevertheless it demands a close reading of the text.

Lastly, the point of view expressed by Professor Vinaver remains: traditional methods of *explication de texte* over-rationalize both the methods and the very concept of the literature to which it is applied. Indeed he goes so far as to say that no educated Frenchman would dream of applying to great works of literature the methods he had learned at school. This is because, in its furthest origin, *explication de texte* was an attempt to understand meaning, and, in rhetorical terms, an attempt to teach elegant writing. It was never intended, argues Vinaver, to teach literary values.

These are serious criticisms indeed but I wish to argue that a less rigid form of commentary has a place in teaching, as one of the weapons in our armoury. It can make important points and instil certain attitudes with force and economy. It would not be difficult to argue that, in spite of the ever-increasing number of books published, there is a growing illiteracy to which the mass media add considerably. Shorthand and speed writing are now supplemented by speed reading, a much publicized method of teaching people to read fast. But how can one *understand Madame Bovary* if, trained in speed reading, one can read it in two hours? After all, Flaubert took four years and nine months to write it. The poet may evolve his poem at snail's pace; sometimes, like Paul Valéry, over a period of years. How can we grasp its almost infinitely subtle developments if we read it in five minutes? Commentary demands slow reading and re-reading; the old-fashioned virtues of understanding and interpretation cannot be better taught and practised.

The attention which we must pay to the words of a passage reveals the powerful resources of language, for it is used to its highest power in literature. One can illustrate the force of irony as demonstrated by Voltaire in *Candide*, in this sentence describing a 'bel auto-da-fé': 'Il était décidé par l'Université de Coïmbre que le spectacle de quelques personnes brûlées à petit feu, en grande cérémonie, est un secret infaillible pour empêcher la terre de trembler'. The culinary undertones of 'brûlées à petit feu' are irresistibly comic, the juxtaposition with the University of Coïmbre is totally deflationary of dogma. The imaginative illumination of the image can be shown. How do you convey the idea of boredom? There comes a point when the idea of boredom can no longer be expressed by variations on the words 'I am bored', 'very bored', 'extremely bored' and you turn to images like 'bored to tears' or 'bored to death'. But here is Baudelaire on the same subject:

> Je suis comme le roi d'un pays pluvieux
> Riche, mais impuissant, jeune et pourtant très vieux

and:

> J'ai plus de souvenirs que si j'avais mille ans.

Commentary is obviously a shorter exercise, in terms of time expended, than the study of a set book. It is therefore a precious way of extending the syllabus by introducing authors who are not 'prescribed'. One can select passages dealing with similar experiences or ideas for comparison and contrast. No syllabus can even approach completeness so that the acquisition of a method, firmly practised, can provide the opportunity of approaching new authors with some confidence.

I gratefully acknowledge permission from Editions Gallimard, Paris to quote the extracts from J.-P. Sartre's *Les Mains sales* and from A. Camus's *La Peste*. During the courses much help was given by Her Majesty's Inspectors: the late W. Ll. Lloyd, at that time Chief Inspector, Wales, Miss E. O. Evans, Miss E. N. Williams, Mr T. R. Edwards, Mr P. H. Hoy, Mr E. H. Hutton and Dr. P. E. Owen. I am indebted to Mr Eryl O. Davies, H.M.I., Chief Inspector, Wales, for his approving Foreword. I owe a special debt of gratitude to the Director of the course, Mr. W. E. Thomas, H.M.I., for his encouragement and constant kindness. Finally, we are all grateful to the members of the courses whose stimulating contributions added much to the discussions.

The Poetry of Baudelaire

CHARLES Baudelaire falls chronologically into the middle group of nineteenth-century poets. When he was born in Paris in 1821 of a cultured, well-to-do father aged sixty and a mother who was only twenty-six, Lamartine was thirty-one, Alfred de Vigny twenty-four, Balzac twenty-two, Alfred de Musset eleven and Théophile Gautier ten years of age. Baudelaire was senior to Mallarmé by twenty-one years, to Verlaine by twenty-three, to Rimbaud by thirty-three years and to Laforgue by thirty-nine years. Heir to a Romantic tradition, his restlessly inventive spirit drove him to question its presumptions; an enervating sense of guilt inspired in him a despair which was mocked by his visions of beauty; a great intelligence allied to a powerfully illuminating imagination, conferred on him a poetic power which has made him one of the greatest and most influential of nineteenth-century poets.

Les Fleurs du Mal, the only volume of poems in verse published by Baudelaire, appeared in 1857. The date of composition of individual poems is not clear but there is abundant evidence that a number had been written considerably earlier. The first edition contained 100 poems arranged in five sections (*Spleen et Idéal, Le Vin, Fleurs du Mal, Révolte, La Mort*), the first section being by far the longest. The volume brought Baudelaire and his publisher before the courts on a charge of publishing immoral and blasphemous poems, thus following Gustave Flaubert whose *Madame Bovary* had been similarly prosecuted—but acquitted—six months previously. Baudelaire was not so fortunate for he was fined and ordered to suppress six poems. In 1861, a second edition appeared with the banned poems omitted, thirty-two new poems added and a new section, *Tableaux parisiens*, in which some of the new poems were inserted together with eight which had originally found a place in *Spleen et Idéal*. The third edition of 1868 is posthumous (Baudelaire had died the previous year) and contains a preface by Théophile Gautier to whom the volume had been originally dedicated. The make-up of the first two editions is important because Baudelaire insisted that the order of arrangement of poems had a considerable significance. He wrote to Alfred de Vigny in December 1861, sending him a copy of the second edition: 'le seul éloge que je sollicite pour ce livre est qu'on reconnaisse qu'il n'est pas un pur album et qu'il a un commencement et une fin'.[1] This is what led Barbey d'Aurevilly to comment on 'l'architecture secrète' of *Les Fleurs du Mal* and to argue that it was not a simple collection of poems but 'une œuvre poétique *de la plus forte unité*'.

The most cursory glance at *Les Fleurs du Mal* reveals a number of startling differences between Baudelaire and his immediate precursors. There is an obvious physical difference. Here there are no long poems, in marked contrast with the normal amplitude of Romantic compositions; this is perhaps one of the most evident proofs of the influence of Edgar Allen Poe whose pronouncement in *The Poetic Principle*: 'I hold that a long poem does not exist. I maintain that the phrase "a long poem" is simply a flat contradiction in terms', was enthusiastically endorsed by Baudelaire. One is reminded of Oscar Wilde's apology to a correspondent for writing an over-long letter because he had not the time to write a short one. Furthermore, there is the rehabilitation of the sonnet whose 'beauté pythagorique' was much admired by the poet although it was a form much out of favour with the French Romantic poets. The national search for an identity which gripped French intellectuals after the Revolution had led to a preoccupation with history, manifested in the popularity of historical subjects in the novel, theatre, poetry, painting and even music. There are no historical poems in *Les Fleurs du Mal*, nor are there any poems based on Biblical or mythological themes. Philosophical discussion is excluded from Baudelaire's verse as are narrative and political poems. It is with Baudelaire that there begins to develop that distinction between subjects suitable for prose and subjects suitable for poetry which takes on a considerable importance in subsequent aesthetic discriminations up to the present time. There is also in the volume a return to the observance of a traditional, classical form of versification for Baudelaire did not follow Victor Hugo in his appeal for liberty from the restrictions of prosody.

These are very considerable differences which will change the course of poetry. Baudelaire consciously fostered the deep originality of vision which he possessed. In one of his projected (but unused) prefaces to *Les Fleurs du Mal*, he wrote:

> Des poètes illustres s'étaient partagé depuis longtemps les provinces les plus fleuries du domaine poétique. Il m'a paru plaisant, et d'autant plus agréable que la tâche était plus difficile, d'extraire la *beauté* du *Mal*. Ce livre, essentiellement inutile et absolument innocent, n'a pas été fait dans un autre but que de me divertir et d'exercer mon goût passionné de l'obstacle.[2]

It is not enough for a writer simply to have the ambition to be original. Baudelaire's private vision of the world and of the human dilemma is supported by a coherent and imaginative theory of poetry and a masterful poetic technique of the greatest subtlety.

6

II

Baudelaire has a sharp intuitive critical sense; he joins Mallarmé and Paul Valéry in France, Samuel Taylor Coleridge and T. S. Eliot in England, as a brilliantly illuminating critic of poetry. One of his most deeply held ideas is stated in *L'Art philosophique* (1859):

> Plus l'art voudra être philosophiquement clair, plus il se dégradera et remontera vers l'hiéroglyphe enfantin; plus au contraire l'art se détachera de l'enseignement et plus il montera vers la beauté pure et désintéressée.[3]

Here he joins Gautier, Flaubert and the school of *L'Art pour l'art* in the belief that art must be *désintéressé*, that is have no ambitions to instruct, to advance dogma or to teach any official morality. Art must be, above all, individual and free. Baudelaire refines this idea in an article on Théophile Gautier, published in the same year:

> Une foule de gens se figurent que le but de la poésie est un enseignement quelconque, qu'elle doit tantôt fortifier la conscience, tantôt perfectionner les mœurs, tantôt enfin démontrer quoi que ce soit d'utile . . . La Poésie, pour peu qu'on veuille descendre en soi-même, interroger son âme, rappeler ses souvenirs d'enthousiasme, n'a pas d'autre but qu'Elle-même.[4]

The denial of the rôle of poetry as moral instruction or as a form of teaching is constant but it must be understood that what Baudelaire is attacking is the view that poetry must be a support of the official morality of the State. Poetry, he argues, must be 'pure', that is, accept only its own standards and aims, remaining apart from other extraneous functions. It is significant that this extract comes from an article on Théophile Gautier in which Baudelaire quotes Edgar Allen Poe's views with deep approval for it is Gautier and Poe who persuade him in this direction. Here is Gautier, in 1835, writing in the preface to his novel, *Mademoiselle de Maupin*:

> Il n'y a de vraiment beau que ce qui ne peut servir à rien; tout ce qui est utile est laid, car c'est l'expression de quelque besoin . . .

and here is Poe, in *The Poetic Principle:*

> I would define, in brief, the Poetry of words, as the Rhythmical creation of Beauty. Its sole arbiter is Taste. With the Intellect or with the Conscience, it has only collateral relations. Unless incidentally, it has no concern whatever either with Duty or with Truth.

We must not imagine that this is to argue that art in general can dispense with all ideas of morality or that pornography and obscenity are legitimate in poetry. Vice is hideous, says Baudelaire, and, since the aim of poetry is the search for beauty, the cult of vice is precluded. The morality of art is an implicit morality:

Il ne s'agit pas ici de cette morale prêcheuse qui, par son air de pédanterie, par son ton didactique, peut gâter les plus beaux morceaux de poésie, mais d'une morale inspirée qui se glisse, invisible, dans la matière poétique, comme les fluides impondérables dans toute la machine du monde. La morale n'entre pas dans cet art à titre de but; elle s'y mêle et s'y confond comme dans la vie elle-même. Le poète est moraliste sans le vouloir, par abondance et plénitude de nature.[5]

There is a further prescription in the sentence: 'Qui oserait assigner à l'art la fonction stérile d'imiter la nature'.[6] There are two important ideas here. Written in praise of cosmetics and fashion, the article points out that nature is cruel and that civilization, in this respect, is a denial of nature. 'C'est la religion qui nous ordonne de nourrir des parents pauvres et infirmes', he writes. 'La nature (qui n'est pas autre chose que la voix de notre intérêt) nous commande de les assommer.'[7] The sentence contains an ambiguity in that Baudelaire is talking both of human nature and the nature that surrounds us. In an article on the painter Eugène Delacroix, of whom he was a great admirer, Baudelaire wrote:

Pour E. Delacroix, la nature est un vaste dictionnaire dont il roule et consulte les feuillets avec un oeil sûr et profond.[8]

If nature is the dictionary, it is art which is the language. The raw materials —sensations, impressions, memories—are provided by the stimulus of nature, but it is the artistic imagination which transforms them. The function of art is not *sterile imitation*. Furthermore, Baudelaire does not share the Romantic admiration for nature and pantheism. In a letter of 1855 to Fernand Desnoyers he wrote, with the irony of which he is a master:

Vous me demandez des vers pour votre petit volume, des vers sur *la Nature*, n'est-ce pas? sur les bois, les grands chênes, la verdure, les insectes,—le soleil sans doute? Mais, vous savez bien que je suis incapable de m'attendrir sur les végétaux et que mon âme est rebelle à cette singulière religion nouvelle, qui aura toujours, ce me semble, pour tout être *spirituel* je ne sais quoi de *shocking*. Je ne croirai jamais que *l'âme des Dieux habite dans les plantes*, et quand même elle y habiterait, je m'en soucierais médiocrement, et considérerais la mienne comme d'un bien plus haut prix que celle des légumes sanctifiés.[9]

These are definitions by negation. When Baudelaire writes more positively, his definitions become more brilliantly affirmative as when he states epigrammatically that 'tout homme bien portant peut se passer de manger pendant deux jours,—de poésie, jamais'.[10] His defence of what poetry really is depends in part on Edgar Allen Poe and it is in a close adaptation of the American poet's views that he explains why man cannot do without poetry:

> C'est cet admirable, cet immortel instinct du Beau qui nous fait considérer la Terre et ses spectacles comme un aperçu, comme une *correspondance* du Ciel. La soif insatiable de tout ce qui est au delà, et que révèle la vie, est la preuve la plus vivante de notre immortalité. C'est à la fois par la poésie et à *travers* la poésie, par et à *travers* la musique, que l'âme entrevoit les splendeurs situées derrière le tombeau.[11]

This is a key passage and to understand it one has to take into account Baudelaire's view of the nature of man. There are, he argues, two opposing tendencies in man and *Les Fleurs du Mal* is in one sense, the history of Baudelaire's own struggles with these two contradictory pulls. He believes in the doctrine of Original Sin which is in us all and, indeed, argues that true civilization is to be found not 'dans le gaz, ni dans la vapeur, ni dans les tables tournantes, elle [la civilization] est dans la diminution des traces du péché originel'.[12] He notes in his diary:

> Il y a dans tout homme, à toute heure, deux postulations simultanées, l'une vers Dieu, l'autre vers Satan. L'invocation à Dieu, ou spiritualité, est un désir de monter en grade; celle de Satan, ou animalité, est une joie de descendre.[13]

Man's inherent urge to sin, implicit in the doctrine of Original Sin, is powerful and pleasant ('*joie* de descendre'); the vast mass of men are happy to wallow:

> Pendant que des mortels la multitude vile,
> Sous le fouet du Plaisir, ce bourreau sans merci,
> Va cueillir des remords dans la fête servile . . .
>
> [*Recueillement*]

Animality shows itself too in wine, drugs (the *paradis artificiels*) and carnal love. But man also has the power to envisage *spiritualité*, a vision of the ideal, enshrining beauty, order and art. These glimpses are vouchsafed above all to the poet who suffers from this privilege of sensitivity and intuition. This idea, easily traceable to Romanticism, is expressed in *L'Albatros*, one of his most Romantic poems in its inspiration and ideas, and in *Bénédiction*. The recompenses offered by the glimpses of the ideal are ephemeral; the visions fade and the poet sinks back into a deadly state of non-existence in which he can experience neither spirituality nor animality. This state Baudelaire describes as *spleen* or *ennui*, illustrating it in a close network of images in poems like *La Cloche fêlée* and the four poems entitled *Spleen*, in strong contrast to the earlier poems of the section *Spleen et Idéal*. It is the poet, above all, who is privileged to discover this ideal and the way in which this imperfect world reflects a greater

9

beauty. That man can do this is a proof of his dignity (see *Les Phares*) and his resultant frustrated suffering may become a cause of redemption. Far from being a poet of lust and blasphemy, Baudelaire is groping for a lost paradise which he knows he will never find. Here he reflects an aspect of the human condition which has become, under the name of 'alienation', one of the major themes of twentieth-century literature.

III

It is now necessary to turn to Baudelaire's theories of the imagination because the structures, the themes and the *truth* of his poems all depend, in one way or another, on the vital place he assigned to the imagination above all the other essential poetic faculties.[14] In this respect at least, Baudelaire is the most English of French poets because, in his defence of the imagination, he stands so sharply in contrast with at least three centuries of French writers and critics before him. The traditional *méfiance* with which the imagination had been treated can be illustrated by two examples, one taken from the field of morals and the other from literary criticism. Pascal, following Montaigne, defines the imagination in that section of the *Pensées* entitled *Les Puissances trompeuses*:

> Imagination—C'est cette partie décevante dans l'homme, cette maîtresse d'erreur et de fausseté, et d'autant plus fourbe qu'elle ne l'est pas toujours; car elle serait règle infaillible de vérité, si elle l'était infaillible du mensonge. Mais, étant le plus souvent fausse, elle ne donne aucune marque de sa qualité, marquant du même caractère le vrai et le faux.[15]

Pascal recognizes the power of the imagination, that 'ennemie de la raison', over all men. He gives a dramatic example. Imagine, he says, the wisest of men placed on a wide, stout plank spanning a great abyss; no matter how forcefully his reason reassures him that he is completely safe, his imagination will override it and he will shake and sweat in terror. Pascal describes the imagination as a 'superbe puissance', investing the adjective with all its seventeenth-century resonances of 'élevée', 'vaine', 'orgueilleuse', 'arrogante'. Its power is frightening: 'L'imagination dispose de tout; elle fait la beauté, la justice et le bonheur qui est le tout du monde'. How close this is to Baudelaire's own views! But Pascal makes a very sharp distinction: the power of the imagination may dominate the reason but it is divorced from the perception of truth. It presents to us with equal vivid force and persuasiveness both that which is true and that which is false. It is not an instrument of moral discrimination and therefore, since it is more powerful than reason, overcomes the very instrument which enables man to unravel the differentiations between motives which should govern his conduct. Here we are very far from Baudelaire.

10

The attack on the rôle of the imagination in literature as conducted in the seventeenth and eighteenth centuries in France is abundantly documented. The classic text is to be found in Boileau's *Art poétique*:

> Un poème excellent, où tout marche et se suit
> N'est pas de ces travaux qu'un caprice produit:
> Il veut du temps, des soins; et ce pénible ouvrage
> Jamais d'un écolier ne fut l'apprentissage.[16]

The passage goes on to condemn the imagination, a 'caprice', as a 'beau feu' (with all that this description contains of something showy, destructive and, above all, short lived) and a 'muse déréglée'. It is rather a description of the *fancy* than of the grave, magical powers of the imagination.

These views are infinitely distant from those of Baudelaire. He conceives the imagination as almost a physical quality without which poetry is not possible. On 20 December 1855, he wrote to his mother:

> J'ai vécu comme une bête féroce, comme un chien mouillé. Et cela durera éternellement, jusqu'à ce que mon imagination s'évanouisse avec ma santé.

But the imagination needs, as its agent of communication, all the resources of craftsmanship and technique to allow it to 'briller de tout son éclat'. It does not exist in a void, the raw materials on which it works are the observations made by the poet on the external world and the play of his senses preserved by his memory:

> Tout l'univers visible n'est qu'un magasin d'images et de signes auxquels l'imagination donnera une place et une valeur relative; c'est une espèce de pâture que l'imagination doit digérer et transformer. Toutes les facultés de l'âme humaine doivent être subordonnées à l'imagination, qui les met en réquisition toutes à la fois.[17]

There is much here to enlighten us. Since art is not the imitation of nature, pure superficial description of the external world is not the rôle of poetry. The sonnet *Correspondances*, which I shall discuss later, states that reality lies hidden behind appearance and so the 'magasin d'images et de signes' which is the world, conceals a mysterious meaning which it is the poet's task, in his rôle as 'traducteur' and 'déchiffreur', to decipher. It is important to note at once that these objects which can bear a heavy weight of significance are in no way rare and esoteric but commonplace.

There is a well-known passage which defines the function of the imagination in the clearest way. It comes from the *Salon de 1859* in which Baudelaire speculates profoundly on its nature and its unique importance in poetry:

> Mystérieuse faculté que cette reine des facultés! Elle touche à toutes les autres; elle les excite, elle les envoie au combat. Elle leur ressemble quelquefois au point de se

11

confondre avec elles, et cependant elle est toujours bien elle-même, et les hommes qu'elle n'agite pas sont facilement reconnaissables à je ne sais quelle malédiction qui dessèche leurs productions comme le figuier de l'Evangile.

Elle est l'analyse, elle est la synthèse; et cependant des hommes habiles dans l'analyse et suffisament aptes à faire un résumé peuvent être privés d'imagination. Elle est cela, et elle n'est pas tout à fait cela. Elle est la sensibilité, et pourtant il y a des personnes très-sensibles, trop sensibles peut-être, qui en sont privées. C'est l'imagination qui a enseigné à l'homme le sens moral de la couleur, du contour, du son et du parfum. Elle a créé, au commencement du monde, l'analogie et la métaphore. Elle décompose toute la création, et, avec les matériaux amassés et disposés suivant des règles dont on ne peut trouver l'origine que dans le plus profond de l'âme, elle crée un monde nouveau, elle produit la sensation du neuf. Comme elle a créé le monde (on peut bien dire cela, je crois, même dans un sens religieux), il est juste qu'elle le gouverne. Que dit-on d'un guerrier sans imagination? Qu'il peut faire un excellent soldat, mais que, s'il commande des armées, il ne fera pas de conquêtes. Le cas peut se comparer à celui d'un poète ou d'un romancier qui enlèverait à l'imagination le commandement des facultés pour le donner, par exemple, à la connaissance de la langue ou à l'observation des faits. Que dit-on d'un diplomate sans imagination? Qu'il peut très-bien connaître l'histoire des traités et des alliances dans le passé, mais qu'il ne devinera pas les traités et les alliances contenus dans l'avenir. D'un savant sans imagination? Qu'il a appris tout ce qui, ayant été enseigné, pouvait être appris, mais qu'il ne trouvera pas les lois non encore devinées. L'imagination est la reine du vrai, et le *possible* est une des provinces du vrai. Elle est positivement apparentée avec l'infini.[18]

The extent to which Baudelaire awards a position of centrality to the creative gift of imagination in all branches of human endeavour emerges here without ambiguity. It is the catalytic agent which activates thought, in its absence there is total intellectual sterility. It has two contradictory functions which complement each other: it first decomposes the world and then recreates it in a new form. In this way it has the power to override accepted ideas so that the poet may look afresh at the world and present a new vision. The act of dissociation is the first step by which the poet, like God, creates a new world. The imagination, 'la reine des facultés', will perceive truth by intuition and, if the products of the imagination are artistically beautiful, then we can accept this truth without question. Evil and vice deform so they cannot lie behind art. This is how Baudelaire answers Pascal's attack on the imagination as an unreliable moral guide.

It is this breathtaking vision of the imagination as creation and as a mode of knowledge which informs Baudelaire's writing. A new drive is imparted to poetry which is still at work. André Breton's first *Manifeste du Surréalisme* (1924) makes the same claims for the imagination and Surrealism represents a movement devoted to the cult of this faculty to an extent which would have astonished Baudelaire himself. This is how Breton describes how conformity in education contributes to the killing of the imagination:

Cette imagination qui n'admettait pas de bornes, on ne lui permet plus d'exercer que selon les lois d'une utilité arbitraire; elle est incapable d'assumer longtemps ce rôle inférieur et, aux environs de la vingtième année, préfère, en général, abandonner l'homme à son destin sans lumière.[19]

The phrase 'destin sans lumière' is very Baudelairean; its use is a testimony to another aspect of his continuing influence.

IV

These subtle and fertile theories evolved as did Baudelaire's experience of the practice of poetry and his discussions of painting and music for he is a questioning, self-conscious poet. One of the most discussed of his poems, giving rise to wide aesthetic speculation is his sonnet *Correspondances*:

La Nature est un temple où de vivants piliers
Laissent parfois sortir de confuses paroles;
L'homme y passe à travers des forêts de symboles
Qui l'observent avec des regards familiers.

Comme de longs échos qui de loin se confondent
Dans une ténébreuse et profonde unité,
Vaste comme la nuit et comme la clarté,
Les parfums, les couleurs et les sons se répondent.

Il est des parfums frais comme des chairs d'enfants,
Doux comme les hautbois, verts comme les prairies,
—Et d'autres, corrompus, riches et triomphants,

Ayant l'expansion des choses infinies,
Comme l'ambre, le musc, le benjoin et l'encens
Qui chantent les transports de l'esprit et des sens.

The belief that all things on earth are a *correspondance* of heaven is very ancient and forms an essential ingredient in mystical thought. Ideas such as these lie tantalizingly behind the text but it would be a mistake to consider the poem as a metaphysical attempt, however compressed, to explain the universe. Jean Prévost has pointed out that 'les correspondances poétiques *ont toujours l'homme pour centre*: elles créent une nouvelle espèce de mythologie'.[20] For Baudelaire, *correspondances* are essentially a new poetic resource, a method of invention which opens to the poet new areas and new methods of intuitive comprehension. The poem became almost a sacred text for it was from the third line that Jean Moréas took the word *symbole* from which the name *Symbolisme* was derived. From this evolved a poetic mode which proved central to poetry in Europe and America. There are two kinds of *correspondances* in the poem: vertical, in the Swedenborgian sense of a *correspondance* between earth and heaven, and horizontal, in the sense of synaesthesia, expressing one sense-impression in terms of another sense. This means of knowledge is intuitive rather than rational and, in Baudelaire's view, is available to the poet because of his gift of imagination. The objects perceived by the poet can become *correspondances* and so conceal a weight of meaning which the poet will convey in terms of images. The first quatrain of the sonnet with its vertical *correspondances* describes these objects in a number of significant ways. 'La Nature' should not be understood exclusively in the Romantic sense but should be extended to include the city and all the appurtenances of modern life for Baudelaire is also an urban poet, the first poet of the city as Balzac was its first great novelist. The 'piliers' are 'vivants', they constantly surround us, are not rare or esoteric, we do not need to be in a state of grace to apprehend them. The words they speak occasionally ('parfois') are 'confuses': their interpretation is not easy and can only be seen by the creative use of the imagination, which is the agent to discover *correspondances*. There are 'forêts de symboles': they are numerous and even commonplace. The key word is perhaps 'familiers': Baudelaire here insists that poetic perception can exercise itself on the most ordinary aspects of life. The subjects of poetry need not be esoteric, illumination can come from the most unlikely source; this is the sense of the last lines of *Le Soleil* (*Tableaux parisiens*):

> Quand, ainsi qu'un poète, il [le soleil] descend dans les villes,
> Il ennoblit le sort des chose les plus viles,
> Et s'introduit en roi, sans bruit et sans valets,
> Dans tous les hôpitaux et dans tous les palais.

The second type of *correspondance* is horizontal, synaesthesia. This is a witness to the unity of the world for 'les parfums, les couleurs et les sons se répondent'. The synaesthesia moves from a *correspondance* between the senses (perfumes which are 'frais comme des chairs d'enfants,/Doux comme les hautbois, verts comme les prairies') to embrace a wider range of reference ('corrompus, riches et triomphants'). The sonnet points to a vast increase in the poet's armoury, by the use of the image not only as decoration but as a means of knowledge.

This belief in the validity of *correspondances* as an intuitive means of understanding and defining heightens the poet's awareness of the world around him. Analogies spring to the poet's mind and are codified in

14

images or in objects. The use of the image in language is as old as speech itself and some metaphors have been used so long that they have become dead. No one saying 'the leg of a chair' or 'the bed of a river' is now conscious of the metaphor although Surrealist artists obtained many startling effects by resurrecting the two elements of the dead metaphor into literal life. The rôle of the image is two-fold, to bring precision and emphasis. To say that 'he runs fast' is almost meaningless because the word 'fast' does not contain a generally agreed measure of speed; to qualify 'fast' by saying 'he runs quite fast', 'very fast' or 'extremely fast', is no more helpful. We therefore invoke a comparison with a measurement of speed we assume to be commonly known and say 'he runs like a hare', thereby making our statement clear. The rôle of the image for emphasis springs from our need to communicate convincingly and to decorate our speech by avoiding the obvious. To say that 'the girl I love is beautiful' may be a personal statement of a sincerely held belief but it is not as illuminating as saying 'my love is like a red red rose'. Language is not possible without the use of imagery.

It is in his use of imagery that Baudelaire has bequeathed to modern poetry one of its most precious gifts, as T. S. Eliot noted in his introduction to Baudelaire's *Intimate Journals* published in 1930:

> It is not merely in the use of imagery of common life, not merely in the use of imagery of the sordid life of a great metropolis, but in the elevation of such imagery to the *first intensity*—presenting it as it is, and yet making it represent something much more than itself—that Baudelaire has created a mode of release and expression for other men.

So it is that Baudelaire widens the range of image far beyond what had previously been judged to be 'poetic'. It is remarkable that in the seventeenth century which witnessed in France an explosion of genius, that writers, from the greatest to the most pedestrian, use a common stock of imagery in which the pains and pleasures of love are expressed in terms of fire or of imprisonment. If the Romantic poets tentatively enlarged the range of images available to writers, it is Baudelaire who goes furthest towards abolishing traditional views of what is 'poetic' and what is not. My love may be 'like a red, red rose' but in *Une Charogne* the decaying body of a dog can also reflect an aspect of the experience of human love. In the poem *Spleen* ('J'ai plus de souvenirs que si j'avais mille ans') a series of trivial objects bear an immense weight of significance, held in a tight poetic tension to recreate that state in which

> L'ennui, fruit de la morne incuriosité,
> Prend les proportions de l'immortalité.

15

A poem can then be composed of objects which stand for something else. This definition of the symbol represents the lesson which Baudelaire taught. *La Chevelure* and *Le Cygne* incorporate into an unbreakable whole a range of objects into a poetic statement whose poetic resonances absorb the reader totally.

One of the great controversies of nineteenth and twentieth-century poetry has been over the question of fixed verse (*vers régulier*) and free verse (*vers libre*). The first lines of Hugo's play *Hernani* produced a near riot at its first performance in 1830.

> Serait-ce déjà lui? C'est bien à l'escalier
> Dérobé . . .

may not be a very good line of poetry but this flagrant *enjambement* of 'l'escalier / Dérobé' was rightly taken as a challenge to accepted verse forms and the harbinger of all kinds of Romantic excesses against good order and literary discipline. Hugo's defence of a *vers libéré* was taken up and ended in the free verse of some Symbolist poets but Théophile Gautier and Baudelaire stood out. In the *Salon de 1859* Baudelaire defended the fixed verse forms in this way:

> il est évident que les rhétoriques et les prosodies ne sont pas des tyrannies inventées arbitrairement, mais une collection de règles réclamées par l'organisation même de l'être spirituel. Et jamais les prosodies et les rhétoriques n'ont empêché l'originalité de se produire distinctement. Le contraire, à savoir qu'elles ont aidé l'éclosion de l'originalité, serait infiniment plus vrai.[21]

The acceptance of the tough discipline of formal metrics was accepted by Mallarmé and by Paul Valéry, whose subtle defence was largely based on Baudelaire's views. The American poet, Robert Frost, when asked if he liked free verse, replied tersely that he preferred playing tennis with a net. Baudelaire is also interested in the tough, restricted form of the sonnet which had undergone a prolonged period of unpopularity during the Romantic period. In a letter of 1860, he wrote:

> Quel est donc l'imbécile . . . qui traite si légèrement le Sonnet et n'en voit pas la beauté pythagorique? Parce que la forme est contraignante, l'idée jaillit plus intense. Tout va bien au Sonnet, la bouffonnerie, la galanterie, la passion, la rêverie, la méditation philosophique. Il y a là la beauté du métal et du minéral bien travaillés. Avez-vous observé qu'un morceau du ciel, aperçu par un soupirail, ou entre deux cheminées, deux rochers, ou par une arcade, etc. . . . ., donnait une idée plus profonde de l'infini qu'un grand panorama vu du haut d'une montagne? Quant aux longs poèmes, nous savons ce qu'il faut en penser; c'est la ressource de ceux qui sont incapables d'en faire de courts![22]

16

V

Les Fleurs du Mal with its secret architecture is a prolonged reflection on the human condition. The prefatory poem *Au lecteur* sets the tone. The line

– Hypocrite lecteur, – mon semblable, – mon frère!

which is quoted integrally by T. S. Eliot in *The Waste Land* confirms the identity of poet and reader in a sometimes compassionate, sometimes ironical and sometimes savage intimacy. In the catalogue of sins 'ennui' looms large, the sin of sloth, spiritual, psychological and artistic. *Spleen et Idéal* develops, although in opposite order, the conflicting pulls of 'spiritualité' and 'animalité'. It is not only human nature which is at stake here but also poetic creation. The poet as creator resembles God and his effort towards the achievement of beauty in art is a striving for 'spiritualité', as is evident in *Les Phares*. That this achievement bears its own pain (*L'Albatros*) is one of the ironies of life. These poems reflect the glories and defeats of the poet as well as the nature of art itself. Another side of the ideal for which man constantly strives is the ideal of love. The poems to Jeanne Duval, Mme Sabatier and Marie Daubrun reveal the oscillations between love and lust, the ideal and a sordid reality. The conflict between 'spiritualité' and 'animalité' is never more clear; the 'joie de descendre' distinguishes poems of carnal love and eroticism. Yet the ideal of a human happiness appears in the touching refrain of *L'Invitation au voyage*:

Là, tout n'est qu'ordre et beauté,
Luxe, calme et volupté

touching because, although Baudelaire had the intelligence and imagination to conceive this ideal, he did not possess the moral discipline to achieve it. The poems on *spleen* (it is not very useful to try to distinguish between *spleen* and *ennui*) describe graphically the state of impotence in which all is circumscribed within an unbreakable circle of black despair. The images used in these poems enhance the idea of claustrophobic enclosure: caves, lids, prisons, nets, suffocation. It is a metaphysical state in which evil becomes almost a physical presence. Yet in 'la conscience dans le mal' (*L'Irrémédiable*), suffering is seen as a means of redemption.

Tableaux parisiens, the section added in the edition of 1861, is set in the city. The poet tries to illustrate the human condition by reference to a contemporary world. Here, the tremendous poetic achievement of Baudelaire is to create the poetic tension necessary to elevate the pitiful but previously 'unpoetic' figures of blind men, old women and the flotsam of the streets to the status of symbols of human error and aspiration.

Le Vin, a short section of only five poems, represents a kind of escape, natural enough given the atrocious pain of living. Once again the blessings of wine are not without end. In *Le Vin de l'assassin*, wine enables the murderer to sleep 'comme un chien' but precisely 'comme un chien' not 'comme un homme'. Guilt and the conscience are dulled so that the gain is no more than temporary and is granted only by the sacrifice of the most supreme of human qualities, the ability to suffer.

The section *Fleurs du mal* continues the examination of possible means of escape, first, escape through carnal love, then by drink and now by sin, but under the celebration of vice, the voice of remorse cannot be stilled. The bitter poem *Un Voyage à Cythère* reveals the true horror of this island dedicated to love:

> Dans ton île, ô Vénus! je n'ai trouvé debout
> Qu'un gibet symbolique où pendait mon image . . .
> —Ah! Seigneur! donnez-moi la force et le courage
> De contempler mon coeur et mon corps sans dégoût!

The progression to *Révolte*, the shortest section, is logical. After the failure of escape, comes revolt against the human condition for which God, as our creator, is seen as responsible. There is no doubt about the meaning of the poems for the attack on religion is sharp. Do the poems contain a true indication of Baudelaire's own views or do they attempt to represent more generally the attitude of man? The nature of Baudelaire's religious beliefs has long been discussed but T. S. Eliot's judgment, in the essay quoted above, is perhaps the most impeccable:

His business was not to practise Christianity, but—what was much more important for his time—to assert its *necessity*.

La Mort concludes the volume. It is not the idea of death followed by resurrection but of death as the final escape. The last lines of the last poem, *Le Voyage*, express the ultimate exasperation:

> O Mort, vieux capitaine, il est temps! levons l'ancre!
> Ce pays nous ennuie, ô Mort! Appareillons!
> Si le ciel et la mer sont noirs comme de l'encre,
> Nos coeurs que tu connais sont remplis de rayons!
>
> Verse-nous ton poison pour qu'il nous reconforte!
> Nous voulons, tant ce feu nous brûle le cerveau,
> Plonger au fond du gouffre, Enfer ou Ciel, qu'importe?
> Au fond de l'Inconnu pour trouver du *nouveau!*

The ambiguity of these lines reflects the ambiguity of Baudelaire's poems. From the confident affirmations of Romanticism, we move to the more subtle and uncertain atmosphere of the poet-seer. Guilt and anguish are his companions perceived in the smallest details of contemporary life but woven into a poetic form which renews the language of poetry. If *angoisse* sits on the shoulders of the characters created by Malraux, Sartre and Camus, the source is Baudelaire.

NOTES

All quotations from Baudelaire's works are taken from *Œuvres complètes de Charles Baudelaire*, edited by Y.-G. Le Dantec and Claude Pichois, *édition révisée*, Paris, Bibliothèque de la Pléiade, 1966 (abbreviated to *O.C.*). Quotations from the correspondence are taken from Charles Baudelaire, *Correspondance générale*, edited by J. Crépet, Paris, Conard, 6 vol., (abbreviated to *Corr. gén.*).

1 *Corr. gén.*, 4, p.9.
2 *O.C.*, p.185.
3 *O.C.*, 'L'Art philosophique', p.1,100.
4 *O.C.*, 'Théophile Gautier', p.685.
5 *O.C.*, 'Victor Hugo', p. 709.
6 *O.C.*, 'Le Peintre de la vie moderne: Eloge du maquillage', p.1,185.
7 *O.C.*, *ibid.*, p.1,183.
8 *O.C.*, 'Salon de 1864: Eugène Delacroix', p.891.
9 *Corr. gén.*, I, pp.321–3.
10 *O.C.*, 'Conseils aux jeunes littérateurs', p.483.
11 *O.C.*, 'Théophile Gautier', p.686.
12 *O.C.*, 'Mon coeur mis à nu', p.1,291.
13 *O.C.*, *ibid.*, p.1,277.
14 For a fuller discussion on this topic, see my article 'Baudelaire and the Imagination' in *Modern Miscellany, presented to Eugène Vinaver by pupils, colleagues and friends* (Manchester University Press, 1969) of which this section is a summary.
15 *Œuvres de Blaise Pascal*, ed. L. Brunschvicq. Paris,
16 *Chant* III, *ll.* 309, *et seq.*
17 *O.C.*, 'Salon de 1859', p.1,044.
18 *O.C.*, *ibid.*, pp.1,037–8.
19 André Breton, *Manifeste du Surréalisme, Poisson soluble.* Paris, Kra, 1929, p.12.
20 *Baudelaire: Essai sur l'inspiration et la création poétiques.* Paris, Mercure de France, 1953, p.75.
21 *O.C.*, 'Salon de 1859', p.1,043.
22 Letter to Armand Fraisse, 18 February 1860. *Corr. gén.*, 3. pp 39–40.

SUMMARY BIBLIOGRAPHY

Austin, L. J., *L'Univers poétique de Baudelaire*, Paris, Mercure de France, 1956.
Ferran, A., *L'Esthétique de Baudelaire*, Paris, Nizet, 1933.
Fairlie, A., *Les Fleurs du mal*, London, Arnold, 1960.
Hubert, J.-D., *L'Esthétique des 'Fleurs du mal'*, Geneva, Cailler, 1953.
Jones, P. Mansell, *Baudelaire*, Cambridge, Bowes and Bowes, 1952.
Leakey, F. *Baudelaire and Nature*, Manchester University Press, 1969.
Mossop, D. J., *Baudelaire's Tragic Hero*, London, Oxford University Press, 1961.
Pommier, J., *La Mystique de Baudelaire*, Paris, 1932, repr. Geneva, Slatkine, 1967.
Prévost, J., *Baudelaire: Essai sur l'inspiration et la création poétiques*, Paris, Mercure de France, 1953.
Sartre, J.-P., *Baudelaire*, Paris, Gallimard, 1947.
Vivier, R., *L'Originalité de Baudelaire*, Brussels, Académie royale de Langue et de Littérature françaises de Belgique, 1952.

Baudelaire: *Le Cygne*. A Commentary

Victor Hugo

I

Andromaque, je pense à vous! Ce petit fleuve,
Pauvre et triste miroir où jadis resplendit
L'immense majesté de vos douleurs de veuve,
4   Ce Simoïs menteur qui par vos pleurs grandit,

A fécondé soudain ma mémoire fertile,
Comme je traversais le nouveau Carrousel.
Le vieux Paris n'est plus (la forme d'une ville
8   Change plus vite, hélas! que le coeur d'un mortel);

Je ne vois qu'en esprit tout ce camp de baraques,
Ces tas de chapiteaux ébauchés et de fûts,
Les herbes, les gros blocs verdis par l'eau des flaques,
12   Et, brillant aux carreaux, le bric-à-brac confus.

Là s'étalait jadis une ménagerie;
Là je vis, un matin, à l'heure où sous les cieux
Froids et clairs le Travail s'éveille, où la voirie
16   Pousse un sombre ouragan dans l'air silencieux,

Un cygne qui s'était évadé de sa cage,
Et, de ses pieds palmés frottant le pavé sec,
Sur le sol raboteux traînait son blanc plumage.
20   Près d'un ruisseau sans eau la bête ouvrant le bec

Baignait nerveusement ses ailes dans la poudre,
Et disait, le coeur plein de son beau lac natal:
"Eau, quand donc pleuvras-tu? quand tonneras-tu, foudre?"
24   Je vois ce malheureux, mythe étrange et fatal,

Vers le ciel quelquefois, comme l'homme d'Ovide,
Vers le ciel ironique et cruellement bleu,
Sur son cou convulsif tendant sa tête avide,
28   Comme s'il adressait des reproches à Dieu!

II

Paris change! mais rien dans ma mélancolie
N'a bougé! palais neufs, échafaudages, blocs,
Vieux faubourgs, tout pour moi devient allégorie,
32   Et mes chers souvenirs sont plus lourds que des rocs.

Aussi devant ce Louvre une image m'opprime:
Je pense à mon grand cygne, avec ses gestes fous,
Comme les exilés, ridicule et sublime,
36   Et rongé d'un désir sans trêve! et puis à vous,

Andromaque, des bras d'un grand époux tombée,
Vil bétail, sous la main du superbe Pyrrhus,
Auprès d'un tombeau vide en extase courbée;
40   Veuve d'Hector, hélas! et femme d'Hélénus!

Je pense à la négresse, amaigrie et phthisique,
Piétinant dans la boue, et cherchant, l'œil hagard,
Les cocotiers absents de la superbe Afrique
44   Derrière la muraille immense du brouillard;

A quiconque a perdu ce qui ne se retrouve
Jamais, jamais! à ceux qui s'abreuvent de pleurs
Et tettent la Douleur comme une bonne louve!
48   Aux maigres orphelins séchant comme des fleurs!

Ainsi dans la forêt où mon esprit s'exile
Un vieux Souvenir sonne à plein souffle du cor!
Je pense aux matelots oubliés dans une île,
52   Aux captifs, aux vaincus! . . . à bien d'autres encor!

Publication:

The poem comes from *Les Fleurs du mal* in which it is numbered LXXXIX, the fourth poem in the new section *Tableaux parisiens* which had been added in the second (1861) edition. Composed after the appearance of the first edition of the volume in 1857, the poem was first published in January 1860 in *La Causerie.* It is important to remember that the poem is contemporaneous with the *Salon de 1859* in which Baudelaire reflects most deeply and at greatest length on the rôle and power of the imagination.

General Characteristics:

The poem is written in alexandrines grouped in four-lined stanzas, in *rime croisée, abab,* with alternating masculine and feminine rhymes. It is divided into two parts, seven stanzas in the first part and six in the second. The poem is triggered off by a *fait divers,* the swan which had escaped from a small Paris zoo, together with memories this brings to the poet's mind of others exiled from their homes. Interwoven, in a majestic orchestration of images, is a description of the rebuilding of Paris which took place during the Second Empire. The whole is a meditation on exile, interpreted in the widest sense.

Thought Structure:

The poem is dedicated to Victor Hugo (as are *Les Sept Vieillards* and *Les Petites Vieilles* in the same section) and this has a special significance. Baudelaire admired Hugo as a poet (see 'Victor Hugo était . . . l'homme le mieux doué, le plus visiblement élu pour exprimer par la poésie ce que j'appellerai "le mystère de la vie" '[1]) and Hugo had spoken of *le frisson nouveau* which he judged Baudelaire to have conferred on poetry. But the reason for the dedication is not merely a gesture made to an admired fellow-poet. At this time Hugo was in self-imposed exile from France after Louis Napoleon's *coup d'état* in 1851 and he remained in exile, in Brussels (briefly), Jersey and Guernsey until 1870 when he returned triumphantly to Paris. Baudelaire sent Hugo a copy of the poem with these words:

> Voici des vers faits pour vous et en pensant à vous. Il ne faut pas les juger avec vos yeux sévères, mais avec vos yeux paternels . . . Ce qui était important pour moi, c'était de dire vite tout ce qu'un accident, une image, peut contenir de suggestions, et comment la vue d'un animal souffrant pousse l'esprit vers tous les êtres que nous aimons, qui sont absents et qui souffrent.[2]

Hugo replied in appreciative terms, referring to the depths of the poem, its 'frissons' and 'tressaillements'. The dedication therefore is addressed to Hugo both as master-poet and exile.

In the 1860 version of the poem the poem had as its epigraph 'Falsi Simoentis ad undam' from Book III of Virgil's *Aeneid.* Echoes of the Virgilian version of the story of Andromache, the archetypal figure of exile, run through the poem.

Although the poem is entitled *Le Cygne,* the first stanza centres around Andromache. The thought of this most celebrated of exiles comes to the poet's mind unbidden and his 'mémoire fertile' begins to work on the external world, that 'magasin d'images et de signes', through the imagination. The second stanza describes the rebuilding of Paris and the third stanza the resultant prosaic chaos. In the fourth stanza Baudelaire introduces the *fait divers*, the swan which had escaped from its cage, nervous and anxious on 'le pavé sec', near 'un ruisseau sans eau'. In the sixth stanza, the reference to 'poudre' points the opposition between the swan's natural element and the dry environment. The swan speaks in a typical Baudelairean apostrophe; it becomes a myth and a literary memory compares it to 'l'homme d'Ovide' ironically, for if 'l'homme d'Ovide' is privileged since he can raise his eyes to the heavens, *en connaissance de cause*, the swan's nervous movements are seen as a pathetic parody.

The second part continues the theme of the reconstruction of Paris with its melancholy background of 'chers souvenirs' and memories flood in. The swan is now openly identified with exile, 'rongé d'un désir sans trêve'; the sad destiny of Andromache is invoked. In a remarkable change of reference and association, the 'négresse amaigrie et phthisique' joins the gallery of the lost, as do those who have lost 'ce qui ne se retrouve/ Jamais, jamais!' (this immeasurably widens the meaning we can give to the meaning of exile), the orphans and, in a magnificent last stanza where memory again takes over, the shipwrecked sailors, the captives and the conquered and 'bien d'autres encor'. It is a poem of complex, interlinked themes with a large cast of disparate characters and a variety of different styles, held together in a high poetic tension.

Detailed Commentary:

The dominant verb of the poem is *je pense*. It is the first verb used and occurs four times, with 'je ne vois qu'en esprit' which amounts to the same thing. In its last three occurrences, the verb governs multiple objects ('Je pense à mon grand cygne . . ., et puis à vous,/Andromaque' *11*.34 *et seq.*; 'Je pense à la négresse . . ., à quiconque a perdu ce qui ne se retrouve . . ., à ceux qui s'abreuvent de pleurs . . ., aux maigres orphelins . . .' *11*.41 *et seq.*; 'Je pense aux matelots oubliés dans une île,/Aux captifs, aux vaincus! . . . à bien d'autres encor' *11*.50–2). Add to these the references to the memory ('ma mémoire fertile' *1*.5, 'mes chers souvenirs' *1*.32, 'une image qui m'opprime' *1*.33) and it can easily be seen how the poet has reinforced the mood of the poem as reflection and contemplation. It dominates its mode of thought and everything, every object or personage, fits into this cadre. It permits the wide associations, the disparate nature of his characters, the different styles: all these would clash horribly in a structure based on logical thought and indeed, it would be extremely difficult to imagine any other structure which would accommodate these elements.

Stanza 1: The first character of the *dramatis personae* to appear is Andromache. Wife of Hector, leader of the Trojan forces in the siege of Troy, she saw him killed in battle. Andromache was captured by Pyrrhus and exiled by him to the kingdom of Epirus. Heroine of tragedies by Euripides and Racine, she is the archetypal heroine of all exiles. The 'Simoïs menteur' is the river Simoïs of Troy, 'menteur' because Andromache imagines the tiny, artificial river she had constructed in her exile to be the river by the side of which her husband lay buried in her homeland. The reference is from Virgil taking up the epigraph ot the poem 'Falsi Simoentis ad undam' and bears eloquent testimony to the hunger of regret, the power of the imagination, the hope and despair of all exile. The style of the opening stanza is purely Racinian with its slow rhythm, its majestic and abstract vocabulary, its rhetorical and easily understood imagery ('Pauvre et triste miroir') and its regular versification. The emphasis is on 'je pense' and the subtle resonant harmonies which come from it.

Stanza 2: Andromache the exile springs unbidden to his mind as he walks through the 'nouveau Carrousel' and the poet's 'mémoire fertile' begins to work. Bernard Weinberg has pointed out[3] that the first stanza 'introduces two sets of relationship, one between Andromaque in exile and Andromaque before the exile, the other between Andromaque and the present thoughts of the speaker'. The contrast between time past and time present is constant in the poem and from this emerges a growing sorrow. Change is all around us but the human heart 'remains attached to the former state, resents the present'. Man may become exiled by time from past happiness and old ideals. There is a marked change of style in this stanza from the noble classical to a deliberately prosaic, almost colloquial tone, although the form remains unchanged (but note the *enjambement* between *11.*7–8). The importance of the unity of tone in a single poem had become an important tenet in the French poetic tradition, alongside the abhorrence felt for a mixture of the comic and tragic *genres* and the emergence of the idea of a hierarchy of vocabulary, establishing the idea of 'poetic' or 'unpoetic' words. The deliberate change of style here practised becomes immensely influential and allows poets a freedom which they are quick to embrace. Rimbaud, in his deeply compassionate poem *Les Effarés*, does not hesitate to shock the reader into attention by his use of a vulgarism:

> Noirs dans la neige et dans la brume,
> Au grand soupirail qui s'allume,
>   Leurs culs en rond,
>
> A genoux, cinq petits—misère!—
> Regardent le Boulanger faire
>   Le lourd pain blond.

T.S. Eliot, in a different form of poetic shock, gulls the reader into the expectation of some serene statement about the dignity and wisdom of old age only to write in *The Love Song of J. Alfred Prufrock*:

> I grow old . . . I grow old . . .
> I shall wear the bottoms of my trousers rolled.

Stanza 3: The poet's memory moves to a more recent past, when the 'nouveau Carrousel' was being constructed, with its accompanying chaos of building materials, themselves neglected, 'verdis par l'eau des flaques'. There are no human figures present so that the scene is curiously dehumanized.

Stanza 4: There is here a move further back in time, for before reconstruction, a zoo existed on this same site in which the *fait divers* of the escaped swan happens. It takes place in the early morning and is an oddly cold and quiet scene, with skies which are 'froids', 'clairs', silencieux'. The only active participants are the poet and the swan. The tone is now narrative and the verse is hastened by *enjambement*. The direct object of the verb 'je vis' (*l*. 14) is 'le cygne' but it is not stated for four lines; this delay contributes to the dramatic suspense of the delayed introduction of the title figure.

Stanza 5: The first words are the direct object of the verb 'je vis' in the preceding stanza and, thus separated, are thrown into relief. Nervous and timid, the swan is scratching the dry earth in frustration, its plumage dragging in the dust. Its gestures appear ridiculous because it is divorced from its natural element. There is an insistence on dryness with the 'pavé sec', 'le sol raboteux', 'un ruisseau sans eau'. One sees a link with Andromache and her 'petit fleuve' but the greater tie—that they are both exiled—has not yet been spoken.

Stanza 6: The syntax overruns the stanza and verse form although the alexandrines and rhymes remain regular with an *enjambement* which throws into sharp relief the verb 'baignant' dependent on 'la bête'. The irony of this word ('baignant' is associated with 'eau' rather than with 'poudre') further points the contrast between the plight of the swan and its wild yearning for water. The swan, its heart now bursting with the suffering of longing, speaks; the poet puts into its mouth words which might have been spoken by a human in a similar plight. The poem makes no pretence at literary realism and the words put into the bird's mouth do not strike an incongruous note; it becomes, in the poet's eyes, 'un mythe étrange et fatal'. The words 'son beau lac natal' which Baudelaire uses to describe the swan's state of mind, are heavy with significance. 'Beau' is contrasted with the ugliness of the city in Stanza 3, 'lac' is the element longed for in opposition to dryness, 'natal' introduces again the lost past of happiness and fulfilment, the absence of exile.

Stanza 7: Bernard Weinberg has written of 'l'homme d'Ovide' (*1. 25*):

> . . . for the reader who remembers Ovid's man it [the simile '*comme* l'homme d'Ovide'] has an ironic twist, the nature of the gesture for man and swan being so completely different and the two moral attitudes being so irreconcilable. Ovid's man raises his head nobly towards the heavens to thank the gods for having granted him that special privilege; the swan stretches his head heavenward with a convulsive motion in order to reproach God.[4]

The repetition of the movement is marked by the repetition of 'vers le ciel'. So the first part comes to an end, a part in which we have seen the style adopted by Baudelaire vary from the high register of Racinian verse to a deliberately prosaic tone. The poet has also used narrative and apostrophe. The scenes described all belong firmly to the past and are seen through the interpretative glass of memory.

Stanza 8: The theme of the rebuilding of Paris now returns but what was, in the second stanza, a sadness ('hélas!' in *1. 8*) now becomes an all-embracing melancholy for 'mes chers souvenirs sont plus lourds que des rocs'. All that Baudelaire sees is 'allégorie': this is why straight description does not interest him for it is literally superficial. What does he mean by 'allégorie'? This is the definition proposed by Littré in an early edition of the dictionary:

> Sorte de métaphore continuée, espèce de discours qui est d'abord présenté sous un sens propre, et qui ne sert que de comparaison pour donner l'intelligence d'un autre sens qu'on n'exprime point.

Paris is certainly a 'métaphore continuée'—we have Baudelaire's own word for it—but the Littré definition refers also to a comparison: the object is presented in 'un sens propre' but it is intended to 'donner l'intelligence d'un un autre sens qu'on n'exprime point'. Nowadays, we should call this a symbol but the definition predates the Symbolist movement with its conferment of a privileged status on the word. *Allégorie*, we must conclude, means *symbol* and Baudelaire's attitude in face of the rebuilding of Paris recalls a happier past. He too is exiled in a kind of present alienation which strongly recalls the refrain of Apollinaire's *Le Pont Mirabeau*:

> Vienne la nuit sonne l'heure
> Les jours s'en vont je demeure

The *enjambement* between lines 29 and 30 hastens the rhythm and sets the pace for the remainder of the poem which now, at the command of memory itself, draws other associations in a headlong rush.

Stanza 9: The figure of the swan now returns for the last time, not in anecdotal form but in his allegorical—symbolic—significance. Note how the poet says 'une image m'opprime': it is an obsession and the verb entitles us to see that he is here writing of a long and deeply felt idea. the swan is *grand* because its symbolic stature has been enhanced by its associations; its 'gestes' are 'fous' because of the depth of its grief. In *l*. 35 comes the image (here a simile) which makes clear beyond all doubt, in prospect as well as in retrospect, that this is a poem about *exile*, although the idea of exile is treated in a very wide sense, metaphysical as well as physical. The swan is described as 'ridicule et sublime'. At first sight, the adjective 'ridicule' seems to run counter to the evident compassion of the poem, but Baudelaire here indicates how the insensitive mass of people, the 'multitude vile', will regard his exile, sunk as they are in sin and the unremitting quest for pleasure. But the adjective is paired with 'sublime' and the 'désir sans trêve' which is the hallmark of the exile. The 'désir' is not defined at this point; although the swan's exile is from its natural element, we are entitled to see exile as something moral, psychological and even intellectual.

Stanza 10: The figure of Andromache reappears in a later stage of her sad history, 'Veuve d'Hector' she is now 'femme d'Hélénus', a far less glorious figure than Hector. The style changes and reverts to the classical rhythms of the opening stanza. There is a change of vocabulary too with words used in their seventeenth-century connotation: 'grand époux', 'superbe' (in the sense of 'proud'), 'extase'. The Baudelairean phrase 'vil bétail' removes any trace of parody. The verse too is slow-moving with end-stopped lines. The figure of Andromache reveals Baudelaire's belief that there may be exile from the past and exile from happiness.

Stanza 11: The poem now broadens into a wider canvas, in which sad and indistinct figures jostle in this desperate pageant. With a fine disregard for literary tradition, Baudelaire juxtaposes the figure of Andromache, in all her stately majesty, with the negress. As did Balzac, Baudelaire removes tragedy from the highest social class; despair and tragedy are part of the human condition. The link between Andromache and the 'négresse' is strengthened by the repetition of 'superbe', here used in the sense of 'splendide'. Once more the physical states are contrasted—the mud and fog of Paris with the brilliance of an earlier Africa.

Stanza 12: The gallery of portraits continues to grow. The stanza is dependent on the verb 'je pense' of *l*. 41. The state of exile is now defined in terms which can apply to all ('quiconque a perdu ce qui ne se retrouve/ Jamais, jamais!'), to the unhappy, the depressed, the orphaned. The reference in *l*. 47 to Romulus and Remus, the legendary founders of

Rome, extends the examples in time. Images abound and are noted with sweeping power, 's'abreuvent de pleurs', 'tettent la Douleur', 'maigres orphelins séchant comme des fleurs!'. Here one hears the true, passionate, angry voice of Baudelaire.

Stanza 13: The poem ends with another reference to 'le vieux Souvenir', now given a capital letter as though to widen it to become the ancient, atavistic memories of the human race. The references range wider and wider in a kind of shorthand notation, to vaster categories of the castaways, the prisoners, the conquered. But what about the final hemistich of the poem, of which P. Mansell Jones has written:

> Now appears what is perhaps the most skilful device of all: the gradual descent, an effectively managed diminuendo, a real 'dying fall'; the tone plangently reflective and fading away into the most casual phrase in the poem. One wonders whether a good poem has ever finished so effectively on so feeble a note—*à bien d'autres encor'*[5]

It is indeed an audacious ending to a poem so full of solemn reflections, and yet after the reverberations of disaster in the 'matelots oubliés', the 'captifs' and the 'vaincus' there seems to be no climax possible. This is why Baudelaire chooses to make it an open-ended finish. We too, the readers, are exiled; the poem continues to echo in our minds, to continue its harmonies long after the book has been closed. This daring piece of anti-rhetoric has had its imitators, as T. S. Eliot who greatly admired 'Le Cygne':

> This is the way the world ends
> This is the way the world ends
> This is the way the world ends
> Not with a bang but a whimper   (*The Hollow Men*)

Conclusion:

This poem continues, in a particular way, the conflict between *spleen* and *idéal*. The theme of exile is developed slowly to become a compassionate meditation on the state of man. There is exile by violence (the swan, Andromache, the 'matelots oubliés', the 'captifs', the 'vaincus') which affects some; exile by malevolent chance (the 'négresse', the 'orphelins'); but, above all, there are those who are 'rongé d'un désir sans trêve', those who have lost 'ce qui ne se retrouve jamais'. So all men are exiled, from goodness by Original Sin, from happiness by life and the passage of time, from the ideal (artistic as well as other) by spleen. It is a bitterly sad and pessimistic poem. The 'images' and 'signes' which are called to the poet's mind in this poem come from his own experience: of the city (the swan, the rebuilding of Paris, the 'négresse'); of his own culture (Andromache and her tragic story, the medieval and romantic

28

resonances of the 'plein souffle du cor', the 'homme d'Ovide'); of anonymous humanity (the 'orphelins', 'captifs', 'vaincus'). The gap in the social and literary hierarchy between Andromache and the other characters is bridged by the styles and is further welded together by Baudelaire's deep, compassionate understanding which springs from his own brooding sense of exile in time. The technique which is used is enormously influential. The disparate objects and characters moving through the verse build up a meditation on the human condition which suggests as much as it says.

This is one of the greatest of Baudelaire's poems. It is a splendid illustration of the definition of the imagination advanced by Gaston Bachelard:

> L'imagination n'est pas, comme le suggère l'étymologie, la faculté de former des images de la réalité; elle est la faculté de former des images qui dépassent la réalité, qui *chantent* la réalité. Elle est une faculté de surhumanité.[6]

NOTES

[1] *O.C.*, 'Reflections sur quelquesuns de mes contemporains: Victor Hugo', pp.703–4.
[2] *O.C.*, pp.1,537–8.
[3] 'A Statement of method: Baudelaire's *Le Cygne*' in *The Limits of Symbolism*, Chicago and London, University of Chicago Press, 1966, pp.16 *et seq.*
[4] *Op. cit.*, p.23.
[5] 'Baudelaire's Poem: *Le Cygne*' in *The Assault on French Literature*, Manchester University Press, 1963, p.128.
[6] *L'Eau et les rêves*, Paris, Corti, 1947, p.23.

Jean-Paul Sartre and 'Les Mains Sales'

IT is not possible to consider Jean-Paul Sartre's work in isolation from the political and social history of his age. This most intelligently polemical man, philosopher and writer, born in 1905, has never ceased to face the challenge of his times, to test in his own conscience the rôle and responsibilities of man as a moral and political creature in the cruel upheavals of the century. Trained traditionally as a philosopher in the Ecole Normale Supérieure, coming first in the *agrégation* in 1929, he became a schoolmaster and seemed destined to become a University Professor of Philosophy. His first published philosophical works (*L'Imagination*, 1936; *Esquisse d'une théorie des émotions*, 1939; *L'Imaginaire: psychologie phénoménologique de l'imagination*, 1940; *L'Etre et le néant: essai d'ontologie phénoménologique*, 1943) reveal Sartre's break with Idealism in favour of broadly interpreted phenomenology. His experience in the second world war and subsequent captivity taught him, he confessed, the rôle of heroism in man and brought him out of abstraction face to face with the tragic meaning of life and, eventually, to an attempt to formulate a methodology, as seen in *L'Existentialisme est un humanisme*, 1946 and *La Critique de la raison dialectique* of 1960. His first essays as a writer were in the field of fiction; his novels and short stories are confined to the decade 1939-49, beginning with the remarkable novel *La Nausée*, 1939. In the same year appeared *Le Mur*, a volume of short stories. His long-projected novel of the intellectual and political issues of the late thirties and war years, *Les Chemins de la liberté*, appeared at the end of the war; the first and second volumes, *L'Age de raison* and *Le Sursis* in 1945, the third, *La Mort dans l'âme*, in 1949. The fourth and final volume *La Dernière chance*, was never completed although extracts from it were published in Sartre's monthly review, *Les Temps modernes*, in the November and December numbers of 1949. Sartre then abandoned the novel to turn to the theatre for which he had first written in 1942. When asked later why he had abandoned the novel as a form, he simply replied: 'Je n'en éprouvais plus le besoin. Un écrivain est toujours un homme qui a plus ou moins choisi l'imaginaire: il lui faut une certaine dose de fiction'; the theatre, he went on to argue, 'c'est encore autre chose. Pour moi, c'est essentiellement un mythe'.[1]

His first play, *Les Mouches*, was performed in 1942 and there followed in rapid succession *Huis-clos* (1944), *Mort sans sépulture* (1946), *La Putain respectueuse* (1946), *Les Mains sales* (1948), *Le Diable et le bon Dieu* (1951), *Nekrassov* (1955), *Les Séquestrés d'Altona* (1959) and *Les Troyennes* (1965). Sartre felt that the theatre had an immediacy of impact which suited his need for communication. It would be quite wrong to describe his plays as 'philosophical' or as attempts to dramatize a philosophical system but they do reinforce his philosophical preoccupations by placing characters in situations which pose the problem of human existence in the terms in which Sartre sees them, both philosophically and morally. These characters too have a sort of family likeness in their lucid search for answers, however anguished their situation may be. This is how Sartre explained the relationship between philosophy and the theatre in 1960 (dates are important because of the honest evolution of his ideas):

> Aujourd'hui, je pense que la philosophie est dramatique. Il ne s'agit plus de contempler l'immobilité des substances qui sont ce qu'elles sont, ni de trouver les règles d'une succession de phénomènes. Il s'agit de l'homme—qui est à la fois *un agent* et *un acteur*—qui produit et joue son drame, en vivant les contradictions de sa situation jusqu'à l'éclatement de sa personne ou jusqu'à la solution de ses conflits. Une pièce de théâtre (épique—comme celles de Brecht—ou dramatique), c'est la forme la plus appropriée, aujourd'hui, pour montrer l'homme *en acte* (c'est-à-dire l'homme, tout simplement). Et la philosophie, d'un autre point de vue, c'est de cet homme—là qu'elle prétend s'occuper. C'est pour cela que le théâtre est philosophique et que la philosophie est dramatique.[2]

If Sartre's career as a playwright now seems to be finished or, at least, to be suspended, it is because his interest in biography and in its methodology has become paramount. The urge to unravel the causes of action and to discern psychological patterns behind human behaviour is a constant whether its mode of analysis be through philosophical treatise, novel, play or in the lives of certain obsessive figures in Sartre's thinking. So he published a study of Baudelaire in 1947, of *Saint Genet, comédien et martyr* in 1952 and has recently, in *Flaubert, l'idiot de la famille* (Gallimard, 1971, 3 vol.), produced an enormously long study of an author whose fascination for Sartre lies in the fact that Flaubert in his almost complete antithesis. We must add to this, the volume of autobiography (*Les Mots*, 1964) which covers his life up to the writing of *La Nausée* and his collected articles and interviews, published under the general title of *Situations* of which nine volumes have appeared down to 1972.

It is not possible even to begin to summarize the evolving complexities of Sartre's thought in a brief space; I shall satisfy myself with an *exposé* of those of his ideas which seem to me to find an echo in the characters of his fictional and dramatic works. The differing philosophies which

31

have been grouped together under the generic name of Existentialism are not French in origin.[3] They can be based on the Christian belief (as in the case of the Danish philosopher, Kierkegaard) or founded in atheism (as is the case with Sartre); what Existentialist philosophers have in common is that their philosophies examine the rôle of man in the world in which he lives and not in abstract, theoretical situations. Sartre explains the implications of the death of God in this way:

En effet, tout est permis si Dieu n'existe pas, et par conséquent l'homme est délaissé, parce qu'il ne trouve ni en lui, ni hors de lui une possibilité de s'accrocher. Il ne trouve d'abord pas d'excuses. Si, en effet, l'existence précède l'essence, on ne pourra jamais expliquer par référence à une nature humaine donnée et figée; autrement dit, il n'y a pas de déterminisme, l'homme est libre, l'homme est liberté. Si, d'autre part, Dieu n'existe pas, nous ne trouvons pas en face de nous des valeurs ou des ordres qui légitimeront notre conduite. Ainsi, nous n'avons ni derrière nous, ni devant nous, dans le domaine lumineux des valeurs, des justifications ou des excuses. Nous sommes seuls, sans excuses. C'est ce que j'exprimerai en disant que l'homme est condamné à être libre. Condamné, parce qu'il ne s'est pas créé lui-même, et par ailleurs cependant libre, parce qu'une fois jeté dans le monde, il est responsable de tout ce qu'il fait.[4]

This is not an easy or comfortable doctrine to follow; far from being permissive, it takes on, in Sartre's thought, an austere and even Jansenist severity. In the absence of any pre-ordained system of divine values which man may inherit on birth, *existence* means to live in a void. It is man's task, if he is to fulfill himself, to attain an *essence*, to live existentially. To this end he will use his freedom, the gift man alone possesses, whose use or misuse is potentially fraught with individual and collective dangers. He did not ask for freedom, it is conferred on him for 'l'homme est condamné à être libre'. The process of achieving liberty demands the foundation of a set of individual values, created from man's situation in the world and this involves also the questioning of existing values and the denial of the past. This explains why Sartre has become more and more drawn to political analysis and, particularly, to the strict examination of communism and Marxism. The idea of man's freedom is a constant in Sartre's thinking. *Saint Genet* develops most fully these ideas; Sartre reiterated his views in a slightly amended form thus, in 1970:

Car l'idée que je n'ai jamais cessé de développer, c'est que, en fin de compte, chacun est toujours responsable de ce qu'on a fait de lui—même s'il ne peut rien faire de plus que d'assumer cette responsabilité. Je crois qu'un homme peut toujours faire quelque chose de ce qu'on a fait de lui. C'est la définition que je donnerais aujourd'hui de la liberté: ce petit mouvement qui fait d'un être social totalement conditionné une personne qui ne restitue pas la totalité de ce qu'elle a reçu de son conditionnement.[5]

Alone in the world, *en situation*, man bears the responsibility of the choices his freedom permits him to make. The anguish of making a choice (*angoisse* is a key word) weighs heavily on him and demands courage whilst its results can rouse feelings of guilt:

> L'homme est seulement, non seulement tel qu'il se conçoit, mais tel qu'il se veut, et comme il se conçoit après l'existence, comme il se veut après cet élan vers l'existence; l'homme n'est rien d'autre que ce qu'il se fait.[6]

The implications of a choice of action will work themselves out throughout a man's life and necessarily influence the lives of others. This makes all the harsher the responsibility we bear for our actions:

> Quand nous disons que l'homme se choisit, nous entendons que chacun d'entre nous se choisit, mais par là nous voulons dire aussi qu'en se choisissant il choisit tous les hommes. En effet, il n'est pas un de nos actes qui, en créant l'homme que nous voulons être, ne crée en même temps une image de l'homme tel que nous estimons qu'il doit être. Choisir d'être ceci ou cela, c'est affirmer en même temps la valeur de ce que nous choisissons, car nous ne pouvons jamais choisir le mal; ce que nous choisissons, c'est toujours le bien, et rien ne peut être bon pour nous sans l'être pour tous.[7]

Sartre accuses those who deliberately choose evil of *mauvaise foi*, they are the *salauds*. Men are *not* free *not* to choose. To be condemned to freedom necessarily means that choice is forced upon us; even if we refuse action, we are still making a choice which will affect others. Thus Mathieu in *Les Chemins de la liberté* is an intellectual so obsessed with the possibilities that freedom confers on him and so fearful of diminishing it by following any one course of action, that he strives to preserve all the options open to him by refusing action. He does not marry Marcelle, but this very choice of refusal positively affects their relationship. Hugo, in *Les Mains sales*, eventually kills Hoederer after a long period of indecision but this does not end his dilemma because he then is compelled to unravel why he committed this act and to decide what meaning it has. It is the mechanism of choice and the complicated motives leading to decision which fascinate Sartre and provide the central situation in his fiction as well as his plays. He describes it as 'un caractère en train de se faire'.

The horrors of the world in which we live are blackly described in Sartre's first novel, *La Nausée* (1938). One of the classics of the twentieth century, it is a casebook of alienation. The central figure, Antoine Roquentin, is driven to the edge of insanity and perhaps even beyond by the incomprehensible hostility of the world. Objects, which should be neutral, begin to take on a life of their own and, in his neurosis, to resist him so that he cannot pick up a piece of paper. This feeling turns to a physical nausea and Roquentin, an intelligent, lucid, university-trained man, seeks to understand his relationship to the world. What he begins to discover with increasing force is that the world has no meaning; there is no principle or order behind it. It is contingent, another key word in Sartre. Roquentin notes in his journal:

> L'essentiel c'est la contingence. Je veux dire que, par définition l'existence n'est pas la nécessité. Exister, c'est *être là*, simplement.[8]

There is no cause or justification for man's existence. Many men accept this and live passively in the absurdity of the world, like cabbages, till they die. Others, profiting by passivity, impose on their fellow men an order which is false because it is designed for the advantage of those who impose it. Those who accept the chaos of the world Sartre calls 'les lâches'; those who try to impose an order on the world for their own gain are the 'salauds'. These are the personages whose portraits adorn the walls of the art gallery visited by Roquentin in Bouville, the town in which *La Nausée* is situated. A hatred of the bourgeois way of life informs Sartre's works. It lies behind his refusal of the Nobel Prize for literature in 1964 (his acceptance would, he thought, make him a member of the Establishment) and his preferred home in hotel bedrooms, as it lies behind Hugo's denial of his own background. There is a savage irony in Sartre's work which is given free rein; Simone de Beauvoir remarks of Sartre and his friends, who:

> dégonflaient impitoyablement tous les idéalismes, ils tournaient en dérision les belles âmes, les âmes nobles, toutes les âmes et les états d'âme, la vie intérieure, le merveilleux, le mystère, les élites; en toute occasion—dans leurs propos, leurs attitudes, leurs plaisanteries—ils manifestaient que les hommes n'étaient pas des esprits mais des corps en proie au besoin, et jetés dans une aventure brutale.[9]

It is perhaps time to open a parenthesis. On many occasions Camus and Sartre have been grouped together in the existentialist camp, to the astonishment of both. Camus said categorically that he was not an existentialist[10] and the bitter argument between them in the late forties over a certain inconsistency in Camus's thought which Sartre had perceived led them irrevocably apart. This did not prevent Sartre writing with his customary honesty on Camus's death:

> Nous étions brouillés, lui et moi: une brouille, ce n'est rien—dût-on ne jamais se revoir—tout juste une autre manière de vivre *ensemble* et sans se perdre de vue dans le petit monde étroit qui nous est donné. Cela ne m'empêchait pas de penser à lui, de sentir son regard sur la page du livre, sur le journal qu'il lisait et de me dire: 'Qu'en dit-il? Qu'en dit-il *en ce moment*?'[11]

34

The fact that both see the world as absurd is nothing, for that is a most inadequate definition of Existentialism. If to deem the world to be absurd is to be an existentialist, Camus observed drily. 80 per cent. of passengers in the Métro are existentialists, if one is to judge from their conversation. There is however a difference in the views of Sartre and Camus on freedom: for Sartre, man is condemned to be free; for Camus, the fact of freedom is in itself a great liberation. For Sartre, this freedom is seen as solitary; for Camus, it is collective. For Sartre, the absurd is ever-present; for Camus, it is to be transcended by collective revolt. Both have a similar attitude to God and agree on the need for commitment, although they define it somewhat differently. Finally, one could say subjectively, that there is in Camus a hope, a flicker of optimism, whilst the Sartrian mode is blacker, more violent, less charitable.

There remains one important question. The writer, too, is a man, living in the same world as his potential readers, condemned to the same liberty and forced to make the same choices: wherein lies his responsibility? It is a question to which Sartre has given a great deal of thought, notably in the long, brilliant and biased *Qu'est-ce que la littérature?*[12] His viewpoint is most densely put in his *Présentation des 'Temps modernes'*, the manifesto he wrote introducing the review he founded after the war:

> Puisque l'écrivain n'a aucun moyen de s'évader, nous voulons qu'il embrasse étroitement son époque; elle est sa chance unique: elle s'est faite pour lui et il est fait pour elle. On regrette l'indifférence de Balzac devant les journées de 48, l'incompréhension apeurée de Flaubert en face de la Commune; on les regrette *pour eux*: il y a là quelque chose qu'ils ont manqué pour toujours. Nous ne voulons rien manquer de notre temps: peut-être en est-il de plus beaux, mais c'est le nôtre; nous n'avons que *cette* vie à vivre, au milieu de *cette* guerre, de *cette* révolution peut-être . . . L'écrivain est *en situation* dans son époque: chaque parole a des retentissements. Chaque silence aussi. Je tiens Flaubert et Goncourt pour responsables de la répression qui suivit la Commune parce qu'ils n'ont pas écrit une ligne pour l'empêcher. Ce n'était pas leur affaire, dira-t-on. Mais le procès de Calas, était-ce l'affaire de Voltaire? La condamnation de Dreyfus, était-ce l'affaire de Zola? L'administration du Congo, était-ce l'affaire de Gide? Chacun de ces auteurs, en une circonstance particulière de sa vie, a mesuré sa responsabilité d'écrivain. L'occupation nous a appris la nôtre.[13]

Here is set out the doctrine of commitment, of *littérature engagée*, to which Sartre has remained faithful. And yet this obsessive writer has periodically come to share the views which Hugo expresses in *Les Mains sales*. The anguished cry uttered by Hugo: 'J'en ai assez d'écrire pendant que les copains se font tuer' finds an echo in Sartre who also feels at times that the weight of a book is not much to throw into the scales against hunger, injustice and cruelty. It is a feeling he has never entirely conquered

35

but in the end of *Les Mots*, a significant title indeed, he finds his only defence. Why do I continue to write, he asks, and answers:

> C'est mon habitude et puis c'est mon métier. Longtemps j'ai pris ma plume pour une épée: à présent je connais notre impuissance. N'importe: je fais, je ferai des livres; il en faut; cela sert tout de même. La culture ne sauve rien ni personne, elle ne justifie pas. Mais c'est un produit de l'homme: il s'y projette, s'y reconnaît; seul, ce miroir critique lui offre son image.[14]

Given Sartre's well-known views on *littérature engagée*, it is not surprising that his novels and plays should have been interpreted as *romans* or *pièces à clef*, bearing a close relation to thinly disguised men and events in Europe. This is a danger of committed literature, that it should be so closely linked to contemporary happenings that when the event has passed and been replaced in the forefront of our consciences by another, the work should become as dead as last year's newspaper. There are two defences against this: firstly, that the literary work should present the event in such a way that it has an application which transcends the merely temporal nature of a piece of contemporary history; secondly, that the literary skill of the author should elevate the subject beyond *reportage* to something more permanent. We must bear these in mind when we judge *Les Mains sales*.

The play was first performed in Paris in April 1948 and was an immediate success with 625 performances. It was produced in the West End in the same year under the title of *Crime passionnel* (the American translation is entitled *Red Gloves*). The French title and its American equivalent are both explained on p.129 of the text, whilst *Crime passionnel* which Sartre considered as an alternative, is also mentioned in the play. It was immediately seen as an attack on the Communist Party and this interpretation became so universally accepted that Sartre went to Vienna in 1954 to forbid its production there. He protested strongly that he had never intended the play to be an anti-communist manifesto and his ban on further productions in the West was aimed at preventing a heightening of political tensions between East and West.

Les Mains sales was written at a time when the Communist Party was gaining considerable strength in European countries. There were many acrid debates on its rôle: should it combine with moderate parties of the Left and Centre to defeat the challenge of the Right or should it abstain from government until it could sweep into total power with the aid of revolution? These debates are echoed in the play in the discussions between Hoederer, the Regent and the *Pentagone*. Communist shifts in policy (see the different interpretations of the assassination of Hoederer advanced by the Party) were seen as a form of treacherous opportunism:

36

these arguments still find their echoes in French elections. The changing relationships between the Communist Party and left-wing writers has been a feature of intellectual life from the Twenties and Surrealism onwards. The humanist, represented by Hugo, is horrified by what he regards as political opportunism and argues for 'purity'. Hoederer's reply is strong:

> Comme tu tiens à ta pureté, mon petit gars! Comme tu as peur de te salir les mains. Eh bien, reste pur! A quoi cela servira-t-il et pourquoi viens-tu parmi nous? La pureté, c'est une idée de fakir et de moine. Vous autres, les intellectuels, les anarchistes bourgeois, vous en tirez prétexte pour ne rien faire. Ne rien faire, rester immobile, serrer les coudes contre le corps, porter des gants. Moi, j'ai les mains sales. Jusqu'aux coudes. Je les ai plongées dans la merde et dans le sang. Et puis après? Est-ce que tu t'imagines qu'on peut gouverner innocemment?[15]

This speech is of central importance for it raises a number of questions. It develops the image from which the title of the play is taken; it poses the question of the rôle of the intellectual in political action; it hints at existentialist views on freedom, choice and responsibility; it considers the implications of government and even has undertones of the bitter quarrels over collaboration which raged in France in 1945 and after. It is this element in the play which seems to me to lift it beyond the question of whether Communism should or should not ally itself with non-revolutionary parties for temporary gain. Hoederer's statement on the wielding of political power—'the art of the possible'—clearly argues that compromise is possible because one cannot 'gouverner innocemment'. Hugo, the purist, cannot accept this 'mensonge': for Hoederer, the fact of 'mensonge' is built into a society which is based on class; to destroy 'mensonge' is not possible unless one first destroys class structure, therefore it is permissible to use 'mensonge' in this process of destruction. It is interesting to remember that the problem of compromise in government is also a major theme in Anouilh's *Antigone*, first performed in 1944. The young Antigone, like Hugo, is an idealist, a purist. Créon, her uncle the king, is, like Hoederer, a mature man and experienced politician whose dialogue with Antigone resembles, in a very different register, the scene between Hoederer and Hugo (*5e tableau, Scène III*). Créon finds himself king, he could have said 'non' but 'j'ai dit oui' and he goes on:

> Pour dire oui, il faut suer et retrousser les manches, empoigner la vie à pleines mains et s'en mettre jusqu'aux coudes. C'est facile de dire non, même si on doit mourir. Il n'y a qu'à ne pas bouger et attendre.[16]

A comparison of these two scenes can be enlightening.

The wider implications of the play, from an attack on Communism, to considerations of the nature of government and the rôle of compromise, are ways in which *Les Mains sales* denies the interpretation that it is concerned with one particular issue at a given time. Another aspect of this transcendence is in the treatment of the revolutionary situation. The theme of revolution has grown in importance in art and literature from the French Revolution onwards and received a great impetus from the Russian Revolution. The first great work to deal with revolution in human and ethical terms is André Malraux's *La Condition humaine*, first published in 1933; a great influence on Camus and Sartre, it is required reading for all who are interested in these authors. In this novel, revolution is the climate in which all the characters live and breathe; it is in this context that Malraux examines their psychology. Are they revolutionaries because they have chosen this course deliberately, in full responsibility to themselves and to others? Is their revolutionary activity a cloak for some unsuspected inner compulsion? Tchen, the assassin, overwhelmed by a crippling sense of isolation from his fellow men, seeks to rejoin his comrades by a courageous act of political murder; in the event, this only emphasizes his loneliness. Ferral, in his activities *en marge*, is shown as interested only in the exercise of personal power; Gisors, the philosopher of revolution, cannot ultimately face the violence of action and takes refuge in opium. Perhaps only Kyo and Katow, who fight because they believe in human dignity, find a harmony of thought action and inner drive. If man is free, condemned to freedom, why did characters of *Les Mains sales* choose revolution? At this level, too, the play transcends the chronicle of a moment of history. Sartre's portrayal of the characters who evolve and take on life as the play progresses, shows considerable subtlety. The existentialist hero, aware of his freedom and responsibility, must choose his course of action in any given situation. Some will choose the right course of action almost instinctively and without question; others will more hesitantly move towards a solution; yet others, like Hugo and Mathieu (in *Les Chemins de la liberté*) never find the answers, for their intellectual debates cloud the issues. In this sense, Hamlet is the first existentialist figure. Georges and Slick, the gunmen protectors of Hoederer, are amongst those who have accepted revolution unquestioningly as a way of life. Their defence of this decision is impatient and incoherent. When Hugo argues that he entered the Party so that all men should hold one another in respect (one is reminded of the insistence on human dignity as Malraux's *sine qua non* of a just society), their answer is less subtle by far:

GEORGES Fais-le taire, Slick, ou je vais pleurer. Nous, mon petit pote, si on y est entré c'est qu'on en avait marre de crever de faim.

SLICK Et pour que tous les gars dans notre genre aient un jour de quoi bouffer.[17]

One almost suspects that they could well fight on the other side, but one has no right to say this because it is a purely intellectual reaction. The total acceptance of the Party and of the rightness of revolution, is to be seen in Olga, who adds intellectual probity to her armoury. Her integrity is such that she is determined to discover why Hugo killed Hoederer: was it assassination in obedience to the Party decision, or was it an unthinking *crime passionnel?* But Olga is also Hugo's lover: had he not, in a final moment of truth to himself, described himself as 'non-récupérable', would she have covered for him? This is an ambiguity which adds depth to her characterization; the comparison with Malraux becomes irresistible. Hoederer is a man of calm affirmation, clear in his views, courageous in his affections, steadfast in his conviction that 'si on n'aime pas les hommes on ne peut pas lutter pour eux'.[18] Hugo is the intellectual who seeks action but who, since his debate clouds his judgment, remains uncommitted in any fundamental sense. The treatment of political themes can often lead to caricature; the typical left-wing portrait of the capitalist invariably gives him a top hat. The nature of the theatre itself leads to exaggeration for any figure on the human scale is diminished to insignificance by the footlights. The theatre demands selection and emphasis. It is a convincing proof of Sartre's dramatic skill that the characters of *Les Mains sales* are subtle, human and far more than political ciphers or stereotypes.

A third way in which the temporal nature of the subject is transcended, added to reflections on government and to the differing attitudes to revolution, is the manner in which the plot is handled. In that splendid book by E. M. Forster called *Aspects of the Novel*[19], there are reflections on the rôle of the plot in the novel which have equal relevance for the theatre:

> We have defined a story as a narrative of events arranged in their time-sequence. A plot is also a narrative of events, the emphasis falling on causality. 'The king died and then the queen died', is a story. 'The king died, and then the queen died of grief', is a plot. The time-sequence is preserved, but the sense of causality overshadows it. Or again: 'The queen died, no one knew why, until it was discovered that it was through grief at the death of the king'. This is a plot with a mystery in it, a form capable of high development. It suspends the time-sequence, it moves as far away from the story as its limitations will allow.

Les Mains sales has a story with a time-sequence made more subtle by use of flash-back, but it also has a plot which exploits both causality and mystery. It is a play of high drama and mounting tension. Will Georges and Slick search Hugo's room and find the revolver? Will Hugo when drunk blurt out his plans? Will he shoot Hoederer? Will he accept Olga's offer to continue with the Party? Is he *récupérable?* All this, with the background of violence, intrigue, guns, cars in the night and, at times, a suppressed sexual tension, give the play almost the melodrama of a gangster film. Yet the play has a high literary quality, for dialogue is more important than action and ambiguities round out the motives of the protagonists.

There is one further way in which the play becomes more than a political play. Since Sartre attributes to the writer the duty of total commitment to the issues of his day, his theatre is an entertainment designed to lead to reflection on our present situation and eventually to the taking of sides. Here Sartre's views on man come to the fore and, in this sense, *Les Mains sales* can be seen as an existentialist morality play. The characters are condemned to be free and they have made their choices which, inevitably affect others. Why did they make their choices? Were the choices made fully *en connaissance de cause?* A number of set-pieces and confrontations enable Sartre to show us how choices come to be made, how an apparently reasoned decision may be affected by temperament, background and even by chance. These all feature Hugo whose lucidity and touchy aggression make him the ideal foil: in his search for himself, he causes others to redefine their position. The sharp dialogues between Hugo and Olga, Hugo and Jessica, Hugo and Georges and Slick, Hugo and Hoederer centre around problems of choice and responsibility. The mixture of dialogue and violent action is not an easy form to handle but this technique contributes largely to the success of the play.

Hugo bears a marked family resemblance to others of Sartre's anguished intellectuals, literate, articulate and impassioned. His rôle as an intellectual in a People's party is a difficult one and his difficulties represent the real conflict of trust which exists between intellectuals and workers in parties of the left. He bears certain superficial resemblances to his creator; their common bourgeois inheritance and their university backgrounds led a number of readers to believe that Hugo was the mouthpiece of Sartre himself and that Hugo's dilemma was also that of Sartre. Sartre has been at pains to dispel this:

Je voulais d'abord qu'un certain nombre des jeunes gens d'origine bourgeoise qui ont été mes élèves ou mes amis, et qui ont actuellement vingt-cinq ans, puissent retrouver quelque chose d'eux dans les hésitations de Hugo. Hugo n'a jamais été pour moi un personnage sympathique, et je n'ai jamais considéré qu'il eût raison par rapport à Hoederer. Mais j'ai voulu représenter en lui les tourments d'une certaine jeunesse qui, malgré qu'elle ressente une indignation très proprement communiste, n'arrive pas à rejoindre le Parti à cause de la culture libérale qu'elle a reçue. Je n'ai voulu dire ni qu'ils avaient tort ni qu'ils avaient raison: à ce moment-là, j'aurais écrit une pièce à thèse. J'ai simplement voulu les décrire. Mais c'est l'attitude de Hoederer qui seule me paraît saine.[20]

Hugo joins the Party in part by reaction against his bourgeois upbringing. 'J'ai quitté ma famille et ma classe, le jour où j'ai compris ce que c'était que l'oppression', he declares roundly to Louis,[21] but this rhetoric—for rhetoric it seems to the down-to-earth Louis who has never felt the need to explain his motives—rings false. It is intellectualized and, in a subtle way, part of what Louis sees as the bourgeois habit of making phrases to cloak reality. Indeed, Louis's judgement on Hugo summarizes the opinion of him held by the majority of his comrades:

> C'était un petit anarchiste indiscipliné, un intellectuel qui ne pensait qu'à prendre des attitudes, un bourgeois qui travaillait quand ça lui chantait et qui laissait tomber le travail pour un oui, pour un non.[22]

Hugo's confrontation with Slick and Georges (*3e tableau, scène III*) reveals the same lack of mutual comprehension. Slick says with considerable percipience: 'On est peut-être du même parti mais on n'y est pas entré pour les mêmes raisons'.[23] Hugo's mounting aggravation as he fails to convince Slick and Georges becomes clear; more woundingly still, his wife Jessica does not take him seriously either:

> Ma pauvre petite abeille, si tu veux me convaincre que tu vas devenir un assassin, il faudrait commencer par t'en convaincre toi-même.[24]

By a deliberate and well-conceived irony, it is Hoederer who finds the words for which Hugo is grasping and the kind of argument most susceptible of convincing Slick and Georges, to patch up the quarrel. Hugo has joined the Party without being driven to it by hunger, a fact which Slick cannot pardon. Hoederer, in his sympathetic understanding, can: 'La faim des autres, ça n'est pas non plus très facile à supporter' and his final formula: 'On juge un type à son travail'[25] is the judgement of a broadminded, humane man. The dialogue between Hoederer and Hugo (*5e tableau, scène III*) is a dialogue between equals. Hoederer does not scorn Hugo because of his bourgeois background; for him, it is rather an argument of principle. If Hugo likes men because of their potential ('ce qu'ils pourront devenir'), Hoederer's warmth towards men is less abstract:

> Et moi, je les aime pour ce qu'ils sont. Avec toutes leurs saloperies et tous leurs vices. J'aime leurs voix et leurs mains chaudes qui prennent et leur peau, la plus nue de toutes les peaux, et leur regard inquiet et la lutte désespérée qu'ils mènent chacun à son tour contre la mort et contre l'angoisse.[26]

The underground alias which Hugo has chosen for himself—Raskolnikoff, the tortured, introspective character of Dostoievsky's *Crime and Punishment*—is typical of his need to pose. But the assassination of Hoederer does take place, in spite of Hugo's growing admiration for him. Hoederer, for his part, has realized that Hugo, having chosen, by an act of reason, to serve the Party, now wishes to act to make himself into the person he has chosen to be. Hugo will only achieve this if he is trusted and the trust which Hoederer bestows on him gives him the courage to act. But would Hugo have fired if he had opened the door at a different moment? Is it really a *crime passionnel* after all, motivated by simple jealousy? In his last discussion with Olga, Hugo says, in a flash of insight: 'Je . . . je l'ai tué parce que j'avais ouvert la porte' and 'Ce n'est pas moi qui ai tué, c'est le hasard'[27] but as the dialogue continues, his mind hardens. To continue to serve the Party after its U-turn of policy would be *mensonge* because he would be an accomplice to its lack of purity. Hugo's deliberate choice of death at the end of the play is, ultimately, to give meaning to Hoederer's end and justification in retrospect to his own life. He is a very subtle creation.

Hoederer is a mature, rounded man of whom Sartre later confessed to his Italian translator:

> J'ai la plus grande compréhension pour l'attitude de Hugo, mais vous avez tort de penser que je m'incarne en lui. Je m'incarne en Hoederer. Idéalement, bien sûr; ne croyez pas que je prétende être Hoederer [. . .] Hoederer est celui que je voudrais être si j'étais un révolutionnaire.[28]

Hugo's attitude towards him changes throughout the play; side by side with his hatred for the politics of compromise exists a growing admiration for Hoederer as a man, real, responsible, having made a choice in life and living it with calm generosity. The unreality of the world, the *nausée*, is absent from him and all he touches. The scene between Hugo and Jessica at the end of the first scene of the fourth *tableau* is significant. Hoederer had made the morning coffee and Hugo is holding the coffee pot in his hands, reflectively. Jessica asks him why he had held *la cafetière*:

> HUGO Je ne sais pas. (*Un temps*) Elle a l'air vrai quand il la touche. (*Il la prend*) Tout ce qu'il touche a l'air vrai. Il verse le café dans les tasses, je bois, je le regarde boire et je sens que le vrai goût du café est dans sa bouch eà lui. (*Un temps*) C'est le vrai goût du café qui va disparaître, la vraie chaleur, la vraie lumière. Il ne restera que ça.
> (*Il montre sa cafetière*)
> JESSICA Quoi, ça?
> HUGO (*montrant d'un geste plus large la pièce entière*) Ça: des mensonges (*Il repose la cafetière*) Je vis dans un décor.[29]

Hoederer has passed beyond despair to hope, the absurdity of the world has been conquered by his choice of love for man. He has become a kind of touchstone against which men may measure their actions. The mode of choice by pure reason is unsatisfactory, choice by action alone is too instinctive, Hoederer confidently uses all his resources. He is, in Sartre's view, the ideal political man of action, with courage but without illusion. He knows that all parties use dubious methods and that Hugo's adolescent yearning for purity is impractical. Hoederer is a practical man rather than a hero, accepting men for what they are and not for what they could be, hiding the truth when necessary, accepting that politics demands violent changes of policy if the final goal is to be reached. Where Hugo is selfish in that he thinks his adherence to the Party will still all his questioning and confer, once and for all, a meaning on his life, Hoederer accepts that life demands a perpetual evaluation of one's choices since one act leads to another. He understands that 'tous les intellectuels rêvent de faire de l'action'[30] but to him action is reality not dream. Above all Hoederer is a generous man, generous in his understanding of Slick and Georges as well as of Hugo. He can envisage his own disfavour and death without bitterness. On Jessica, who has refused to live in the real world, he bestows the gift of life as she readily confesses:

> Je ne sais rien, je ne suis ni femme ni fille, j'ai vécu dans un songe et quand on m'embrassait ça me donnait envie de rire. A présent je suis là devant vous, il me semble que je viens de me réveiller et que c'est le matin. Vous êtes vrai. Un vrai homme de chair et d'os, j'ai vraiment peur de vous et je crois que je vous aime pour de vrai. Faites de moi ce que vous voudrez: quoi qu'il arrive, je ne vous reprocherai rien.[31]

Hoederer's last act of generosity is to spare Hugo's life by his false confession.

Les Mains sales is a rich play, not only in the political resonances of its plot with their relevance for the contemporary world but also because of the austere light it throws on man's responsibility for his actions. Good theatre in its portrayal of character and in its rapid, colloquial dialogue employing different registers of style, it is a disturbing, uncomfortable work which illuminates the human condition in the twentieth century.

NOTES

All references to the text of *Les Mains sales* (abbreviated to *MS*) are taken from the edition by Geoffrey Brereton, London, Methuen, 1963, revised edition, 1971.

[1] 'Sartre par Sartre', an interview in *New Left*, reprinted in *Le Nouvel Observateur*, 26 January 1970. J.-P. Sartre, *Situations, IX*, Paris, Gallimard, 1972, p.123.

[2] Madeleine Chapsal, *Les Ecrivains en personne*, Paris, Julliard, 1960. Reprinted in *Situations, IX*, pp.12–3.

[3] For a general discussion on Existentialism in France, see I. W. Alexander, 'La Philosophie existentialiste en France: ses sources et ses problèmes fondamentaux', *French Studies*, 1, 2, April 1947.

[4] *L'Existentialisme est un humanisme*, Paris, Nagel, 1946, pp.36–7. Originally a lecture given by Sartre in 1945, at the height of the existentialist vogue in France, it had a tremendous success. Philip Thody has noted that it sold 120,000 copies.

5 'Sartre par Sartre', *Situations, IX,* pp.101–2.
6 *L'Existentialisme est un humanisme,* p.22.
7 *Ibid.* pp.25–6.
8 *La Nausée,* Paris, Gallimard, 1938, p.167.
9 *Mémoires d'une jeune fille rangée,* Paris, Gallimard, 1958, pp.335–6. There are many references to Sartre in this autobiography. The second and third volumes are *La Force de l'âge* (1960) and *La Force des choses* (1963) both published in Paris by Gallimard.
10 See 'Extraits d'interviews: Non, je ne suis pas existentialiste', A. Camus, *Essais,* Paris, Pléiade, 1965, pp.1,424 *foll.*
11 'Albert Camus', *France-Observateur,* no.505, 7 January 1960. *Situations, IV,* 1964, p.126.
12 *Situations, ii,* 1948.
13 *Ibid.* pp.12–3.
14 *Les Mots,* Paris, Gallimard, 1964, p.211.
15 *MS,* p.129.
16 Jean Anouilh, *Antigone,* Paris, Didier, Les Classiques de la civilisation française, 1964, p.65.
17 *MS,* p.68.
18 *MS,* p.130.
19 First published in 1927. The quotation is from the edition by Pelican Books, 1962, pp.93–4.
20 F. Jeanson, *Sartre par lui-même,* Paris, Ed. du Seuil, 1955, p.48.
21 *MS,* p.49.
22 *MS,* p.37.
23 *MS,* p.71.
24 *MS,* p.84.
25 *MS,* p.73.
26 *MS,* p.131.
27 *MS,* p.147.
28 Quoted in *Les Critiques de notre temps et Sartre,* ed. Jacques Lecarme, Paris, Garnier 1973, p.21.
29 *MS,* p.90.
30 *MS,* p.79.
31 *MS,* p.145.

SUMMARY BIBLIOGRAPHY

ALBÉRÈS, R.-M. *Jean-Paul Sartre,* Paris, Classiques du XXᵉ siècle, 1960.
RYBALKA, MICHEL CONTAT & MICHEL *Les Ecrits de Sartre,* Paris Gallimard, 1970.
CRANSTON, MAURICE *Sartre,* Edinburgh & London, Oliver & Boyd, 1962.
JEANSON, FRANCIS *Sartre par lui-même,* Ed. du Seuil, Paris, 1955.
MURDOCH, IRIS *Sartre,* Cambridge, Bowes & Bowes, 1952.
PEYRE, HENRI *Jean-Paul Sartre,* New York & London, Columbia University Press, 1968.
THODY, PHILIP *Jean-Paul Sartre, a Literary and Political Study,* London, Hamish Hamilton, 1960.
Sartre, a Biographical Introduction, London, Studio Vista, 1971.
VERSTRAETEN, PIERRE *Violence et éthique: esquisse d'une critique de la morale dialectique à partir du théâtre politique de Sartre,* Paris, Gallimard, 1972.
Les Critiques de notre temps et Sartre, Paris, Garnier, 1973.

Les Mains Sales. Commentary

HOEDERER Sans aucune importance. Nous en reparlerons. (*A Slick*) Qu'est-ce qu'il y a eu? Qu'est-ce que vous lui reprochez? Il est trop bien habillé? Il parle comme un livre?

SLICK Question de peau.

5   HOEDERER Pas de ça ici. Les peaux, on les laisse au vestiaire. (*Il les regarde*) Mes enfants, vous êtes mal partis. (*A Hugo*) Toi, tu fais l'insolent parce que tu es le plus faible. (*A Slick et à Georges*) Vous, vous avez vos gueules des mauvais jours. Vous avez commencé par le regarder de travers. Demain vous lui

10   ferez des farces et la semaine prochaine, quand j'aurai besoin de lui dicter une lettre, vous viendrez me dire qu'on l'a repêché dans l'étang.

HUGO Pas si je peux l'empêcher . . .

HOEDERER Tu ne peux rien empêcher. Ne te crispe pas, mon

15   petit. Il ne faut pas que les choses en arrivent là, voilà tout. Quatre hommes qui vivent ensemble, ça s'aime ou ça se massacre. Vous allez me faire le plaisir de vous aimer.

GEORGES (*avec dignité*) Les sentiments ne se commandent pas.

HOEDERER (*avec force*) Ils se commandent. Ils se commandent

20   quand on est en service, entre types du même parti.

GEORGES On n'est pas du même parti.

HOEDERER (*à Hugo*) Tu n'es pas de chez nous?

HUGO Si.

HOEDERER Alors?

25   SLICK On est peut-être du même parti mais on n'y est pas entré pour les mêmes raisons.

HOEDERER On y entre toujours pour la même raison.

SLICK Tu permets! Lui, c'était pour apprendre aux pauvres gens le respect qu'ils se doivent.

30   HOEDERER Bah?

GEORGES C'est ce qu'il a dit.

HUGO Et vous, vous n'y êtes entrés que pour bouffer à votre faim. C'est ce que vous avez dit.

45

HOEDERER Eh bien? Vous êtes d'accord.

35 SLICK Pardon?

HOEDERER Slick! Tu ne m'as pas raconté que tu avais honte d'avoir faim? (*Il se penche vers Slick et attend une réponse qui ne vient pas*) Et que ça te faisait rager parce que tu ne pouvais penser à rien d'autre? Et qu'un garçon de vingt ans a mieux à
40 faire qu'à s'occuper tout le temps de son estomac?

SLICK Tu n'avais pas besoin de parler de ça devant lui.

HOEDERER Tu ne me l'as pas raconté?

SLICK Qu'est-ce que ça prouve?

HOEDERER Ça prouve que tu voulais ta bouffe et un petit quelque
45 chose en plus. Lui, il appelle ça le respect de soi-même. Il faut le laisser dire. Chacun peut employer les mots qu'il veut.

SLICK Ça n'était pas du respect. Ça me ferait bien mal qu'on appelle ça du respect. Il emploie les mots qu'il trouve dans sa tête; il pense tout avec sa tête.

50 HUGO Avec quoi veux-tu que je pense?

SLICK Quand on la saute, mon pote, c'est pas avec sa tête qu'on pense. C'est vrai que je voulais que ça cesse, bon Dieu oui. Rien qu'un moment, un petit moment, pour pouvoir m'intéresser à autre chose. A n'importe quoi d'autre que moi.
55 Mais c'était pas du respect de moi-même. Tu n'as jamais eu faim et tu es venu chez nous pour nous faire la morale comme les dames visiteuses qui montaient chez ma mère quand elle était saoule pour lui dire qu'elle ne se respectait pas.

HUGO C'est faux.

60 GEORGES Tu as eu faim, toi? Je crois que tu avais plutôt besoin de prendre de l'exercice avant les repas pour te mettre en appétit.

HUGO Pour une fois, tu as raison, mon grand camarade: l'appétit je ne sais pas ce que c'est. Si tu avais vu les phosphatines de mon enfance, j'en laissais la moitié: quel gaspillage! Alors on
65 m'ouvrait la bouche, on me disait: une cuillerée pour papa, une cuillerée pour maman, une cuillerée pour la tante Anna. Et on m'enfonçait la cuiller jusqu'au fond de la gorge. Et je grandissais, figure-toi. Mais je ne grossissais pas. C'est le moment où on m'a fait boire du sang frais aux abattoirs,
70 parce que j'étais pâlot: du coup je n'ai plus touché à la viande. Mon père disait chaque soir: "Cet enfant n'a pas faim . . ." Chaque soir, tu vois ça d'ici: "Mange, Hugo, mange. Tu vas te rendre malade." On m'a fait prendre de l'huile de foie de

morue: ça c'est le comble du luxe: une drogue pour te *donner*
faim pendant que les autres, dans la rue, se seraient vendus
pour un bifteck; je les voyais passer de ma fenêtre avec leur
pancarte: "Donnez-nous du pain." Et j'allais m'asseoir à
table. Mange, Hugo, mange. Une cuillerée pour le gardien
qui est en chômage, une cuillerée pour la vieille qui ramasse
les épluchures dans la poubelle, une cuillerée pour la famille
du charpentier qui s'est cassé la jambe. J'ai quitté la maison.
Je suis entré au Parti et c'était pour entendre la même chanson: "Tu n'as jamais eu faim, Hugo, de quoi que tu te mêles?
Qu'est-ce que tu peux comprendre? Tu n'as jamais eu faim."
Eh bien non, je n'ai jamais eu faim. Jamais! Jamais! Jamais!
Tu pourras peut-être me dire, toi, ce qu'il faut que je fasse
pour que vous cessiez tous de me le reprocher.

(*Un temps*)

HOEDERER Vous entendez? Eh bien, renseignez-le. Dites-lui donc
ce qu'il faut qu'il fasse. Slick! Que lui demandes-tu? Qu'il se
coupe une main? Qu'il se crève un œil? Qu'il t'offre sa femme?
Quel prix doit-il payer pour que vous lui pardonniez?

SLICK Je n'ai rien à lui pardonner.

HOEDERER Si: d'être entré au Parti sans y être poussé par la
misère.

GEORGES On ne lui reproche pas. Seulement il y a un monde
entre nous: lui, c'est un amateur, il y est entré parce qu'il
trouvait ça bien, pour faire un geste. Nous, on ne pouvait pas
faire autrement.

HOEDERER Et lui, tu crois qu'il pouvait faire autrement? La faim
des autres, ça n'est pas non plus très facile à supporter.

GEORGES Il y en a beaucoup qui s'en arrangent très bien.

HOEDERER C'est qu'ils n'ont pas d'imagination. Le malheur avec
ce petit-là, c'est qu'il en a trop.

SLICK Ça va. On ne lui veut pas de mal. On ne le blaire pas,
c'est tout. On a tout de même le droit . . .

HOEDERER Quel droit? Vous n'avez aucun droit. Aucun. "On ne
le blaire pas" . . . Espèces de salauds, allez regarder vos
gueules dans la glace et puis vous reviendrez me faire de la
délicatesse de sentiment si vous en avez le courage. On juge
un type à son travail. Et prenez garde que je ne vous juge au
vôtre, parce que vous vous relâchez drôlement ces temps-ci.

HUGO (*criant*) Mais ne me défendez pas! Qui vous demande de
me défendre? Vous voyez bien qu'il n'y a rien à faire; j'ai

47

115   l'habitude. Quand je les ai vus entrer, tout à l'heure, j'ai reconnu
leur sourire. Ils n'étaient pas beaux. Vous pouvez me croire;
ils venaient me faire payer pour mon père et pour mon
grand-père et pour tous ceux de ma famille qui ont mangé à
leur faim. Je vous dis que je les connais: jamais ils ne m'accep-
120   teront; ils sont cent mille qui regardent avec ce sourire. J'ai
lutté, je me suis humilié, j'ai tout fait pour qu'ils oublient, je
leur ai répété que je les aimais, que je les enviais, que je les
admirais. Rien à faire! Rien à faire! Je suis un gosse de riches,
un intellectuel, un type qui ne travaille pas de ses mains. Eh
125   bien, qu'ils pensent ce qu'ils veulent. Ils ont raison, c'est une
question de peau.
          (*Slick et Georges se regardent en silence*)
       HOEDERER (*aux gardes du corps*) Eh bien? (*Slick et Georges
       haussent les épaules en signe d'incertitude*) Je ne le ménagerai
130   pas plus que vous: vous savez que je ne ménage personne. Il
ne travaillera pas de ses mains, mais je le ferai trimer dur.
(*Agacé*) Ah! Finissons-en.

Introduction

It is not easy to isolate a passage from a play as relatively compressed
and as tightly-structured as *Les Mains sales*. The passage chosen contains
no action and depends, for its success, on rapid interchanges in a style
which reproduces the appropriate speech registers of the protagonists. The
conflict is psychological, revealing the deep suspicions aroused by differences of class origin, but underlying the exchanges are questions of the
implications of choice. Why do we choose one course of action rather than
another? Is Hugo's decision to join the Party as authentic and of the same
order as the decision of Slick and Georges? Is hunger a more valid motive
for political commitment than reason? What does service to a political
party mean? These lie at the heart of what appears to be a simple clash of
temperament leading to immediate dislike. Wider questions about social
justice are raised by Hugo's impassioned speech but the theatrical presentation is vivid and immediate.

General character

This is the first confrontation between Slick, Georges and Hugo. The
rapid increase in tension calls for the presence of Hoederer whose rôle
as adjudicator is seen as important if the small group is not to be torn
apart by clashes of temperament. Hugo and Jessica—as well as the audience
—know that the threatened search of their luggage will reveal the hidden
revolver; the risk of Hugo's threatened exposure adds dramatically to the

movement of dialogue. Yet Hugo's deep desire to be trusted and accepted is clear in all he says. The presence of Jessica, who is silent in this extract, adds a sexual tension. All the men are conscious of her presence; Hugo's self-justifications are addressed to her as much as the others.

Structure

Hoederer begins by attempting to understand the reasons for the quarrel. He first suspects it to be attributable to a clash of class in its most superficial aspects. Slick's brief reply that it is a 'question de peau' rouses Hoederer to a scornful reply in which he verbally knocks their heads together as though they were simply quarrelsome children. His judgment 'Vous allez me faire le plaisir de vous aimer' (1. 17) appears to Georges to be an unpardonable intrusion on his right to his own opinions. This is brushed aside by Hoederer and Georges changes his attack to reveal the real reason for his dislike of Hugo: 'On n'est pas du même parti'. Is the aim of the Party the restoration of human dignity, an ambition reached by the intellectual processes of reason in the case of Hugo? Or is it a more material aim, to ensure that everyone has enough to eat? This, for Slick and Georges, is the conclusion which they have instinctively reached simply by the circumstances of their lives. Hugo's impassioned speech argues that physical deprivation is not the only route which leads to political commitment. Hoederer's trenchant judgment is followed by Hugo's cry of self-pitying frustration. The extract ends with a fragile truce.

Detailed commentary

Although Hoederer's manner and style are brusque, they conceal a considerable sensitivity to personalities as well as to events. Having determined that Jessica is not at the root of the trouble, he at once sees that what is at issue is not the search but an instant and instinctive dislike which he must have come across before in his political work—the deep-seated distrust between intellectual and worker. This worries Hoederer because it can lead to waste of effort and inefficiency. His tone is sharp and ironic, using language that Slick and Georges can understand: 'Il est trop bien habillé? Il parle comme un livre?' (1. 3). He appears as the chief, decisive, blunt, challenging. Slick's explanation: 'Question de peau' is honest if not very intelligent and it in no way surprises Hoederer who is revealed as a penetrating practical psychologist. He sees through Hugo's bluster as the reaction of the weak man trying to *se faire valoir* whilst Slick and Georges, although somewhat cowed by Hugo's superior powers of articulateness, bully him with the confidence of their superior physical strength, a form of masculine assertion in the presence of Jessica. Hoederer's experience leads him to foresee violence and, brushing aside Hugo's feeble expostulation 'pas si je peux l'empêcher' (1. 13), orders them to get together for the sake of efficiency. He uses brutal, concrete language with no appeal to abstraction. The example of 'dicter une lettre' (1. 11) is well within the grasp of Slick and Georges. Georges's statement 'On n'est pas du même parti' (1.21) reveals their naked prejudice against the middle-class background of Hugo. Slick and Georges appear as extraordinarily conservative in their attitude to one from another social class. This has been a common experience for the bourgeois intellectual in the Communist Party and Sartre himself must have experienced it. The argument between the two sides now develops. Is it more valid to join the Party because one has been driven to it by the force of material things or to come as a result of ideological conviction? This is central to the extract. The implications of choice appear here too. What factors does a man take into account when he chooses a course of action? How can he sustain and give meaning to his choice? For Slick and Georges, choice was dictated by naked hunger. To avoid being hungry is a way to achieve dignity, says Hoederer, stating Hugo's case better than he can. Hoederer's powers of understanding see beyond Slick's incoherent protests which end with the significant words: 'il pense tout avec sa tête' (1. 49). Here is all the latent distrust of the intellectual and the conviction that conclusions reached by the process of reason are invalid. This is the central problem which faces Hugo: having chosen to adhere to the Party, he is still not totally convinced that he is able to live with the responsibility which this choice has conferred on him. 'Chacun peut employer les mots qu'il veut' (1. 46), says Hoederer, but Hugo, expert as he is in the marshalling of words, needs trust and action to confirm him in his belief. Hugo is stung to make his passionate speech denying hunger as the only valid reason for the choice of revolutionary action by Slick's percipient remark that Hugo has only come to 'faire la morale' (1.56). It is a piece of ferocious irony, a savage attack on his bourgeois upbringing, recalling similar bitter attacks in La Nausée, reflecting Sartre's own views. Hugo is given drugs to stimulate his hunger whilst outside his windows, people are slowly dying of hunger. There is a cutting edge to his tongue here—Hugo is, after all, a writer—and he establishes a most effective symmetry between the traditional method of persuading a child to eat ('une cuillerée pour papa . . .') and the twisted parody of 'une cuillerée pour le gardien qui est en chômage'. Hugo, the existentialist man, has made his choice from his reason and his conscience; in rejecting injustice, he chooses justice, but it is a choice which remains an intellectual stance and does not change him. Note the later irony when Hoederer discovers the photographs of Hugo's past which he cannot bring himself to disavow. What then, cries Hugo passionately, must he do to be accepted by others?;

50

it is only too plain that he has not accepted his own responsibilities nor the full implications of his choice.

At the end of Hugo's speech there is a dramatic pause. Slick and Georges remain unconcerned for this, to them, is only rhetoric. Hoederer cuts in sharply with a series of staccato questions, concrete, down to earth, using the language of Slick and Georges. He understands that their complaint against Hugo is 'd'être entré au Parti sans y être poussé par la misère' (11. 94–95). To Georges's accusation that Hugo is an amateur, Hoederer replies with a rare piece of moralizing: 'la faim des autres, ça n'est pas non plus très facile à supporter' (11. 100–1). Slick can find no answer to Hoederer's statements, and, impatient with argumentation, says, 'On ne le blaire pas, c'est tout' (1. 105), revealing once again the issue of personality. To Hoederer's stern protestation of faith 'On juge un type à son travail' (1. 110), Hugo cries out in self-pity, revealing his frustration, his failure to make himself accepted, his lack of confidence. Hoederer brings to an uneasy close a patched-up truce. Much has been said and much revealed but nothing has been solved.

Style

The dramatic tension in the passage is clear although there is no physical action. The cut and thrust of argument on different levels, the silent presence of Jessica, the moments when Hugo is talked about as though he were not there (a situation irritatingly insulting to him), all centre around the dominating presence of Hoederer. The styles of speech vary greatly from the inarticulate slang of Slick and Georges to the more literary speech of Hugo. Bridging them is Hoederer who speaks the two languages with ease. The device of *tutoiement* further unifies the dialogue. Apart from the use of *tu* being natural in the context of a Party based on ideas of equality, it irons out any pejorative shades of meaning between *tu* and *vous* and puts all the characters on the same level of intimacy.

Conclusion

The passage does not advance the action for there is no issue here which changes anything. Yet it is a passage of central importance for it broadens and deepens the knowledge we have of Hugo, his reasons for joining the Party, his need to be trusted and his desperate search for self-conviction. It also shows the character of Hoederer in a generous light. In more general terms, other issues are raised: the conflict between intellectual and non-intellectual in the Party; the question of choice, its motives and validity; the condition of existentialist man, his freedom to choose and its resulting responsibilities. When all this has been said, we must recognize that it is simply very good theatre.

Albert Camus and *La Peste*

It is not my purpose to give a general account of the life and work of Albert Camus [1913–60] but rather to discuss his novel *La Peste* which was published in 1947. One of the most widely read books of the twentieth century, it has appeared in translation in twenty-two different countries and, from where we stand now with the lack of critical perspective given by time, it appears to be one of the most significant books of our age. Yet one cannot consider *La Peste* alone. In 1952, Camus was asked whether he would write a sequel to his collection of essays entitled *L'Homme révolté* which had appeared the year before. He replied:

> A certains égards, ce livre est une confidence, la seule sorte de confidence, du moins, dont je sois capable, et que j'ai mis quatre ans à formuler avec les scrupules et les nuances qui s'imposaient. Je ne crois pas, en ce qui me concerne, aux livres isolés. Chez certains écrivains, il me semble que leurs œuvres forment un tout où chacune s'éclaire par les autres, et où toutes se regardent.[1]

This essay will attempt to set *La Peste* against *L'Etranger* and *Le Mythe de Sisyphe*, both of 1942. I shall not discuss Camus's plays on the grounds that the theatre, being a different literary *genre*, poses different problems and suggests different solutions.

II

There is little to delay us in the circumstances of his life. Born on 7 November 1913 at Mondovi in Algeria, Camus was the second son of a French father of Alsatian stock; his mother was of Spanish descent. His father was killed in 1914 in the First World War; the family then moved to a poor quarter of Algiers and Camus has recorded some of his experiences of this time in a series of essays and *récits* entitled *L'Envers et l'endroit* first published in 1937. From the lycée, Camus, a voracious and precocious reader, went up to the University of Algiers to read philosophy. Like J.-P. Sartre, he took avidly to this discipline receiving his *licence* and a *diplôme d'études supérieures* for a dissertation on the relations between Greek and Christian thought in the works of Plotinus and St. Augustine. His preparation for the *agrégation* was interrupted by a renewed attack of the tuberculosis he had first contracted in 1930. The young Camus was a keen sportsman and kept goal for his soccer club. He was also keenly interested in the theatre and, in 1935, had founded the *Théâtre du Travail*, an amateur group with the ambition of presenting plays to a mixed public of workers and intellectuals. He had joined the Communist Party in 1934 but left it one year later because, as Professor Cruickshank says, he was 'never able to accept expediency as an adequate basis for political action'.[2] He travelled widely, becoming active as a journalist. The outbreak of war in 1939 saw him rejected by the Army on health grounds and he joined the staff of *Paris-Soir*. He returned to Algiers in 1941 and to France in 1942 to become a member of the 'Combat' Resistance group. From then on, his life is the history of his work. He rapidly became a figure of international importance and was awarded the Nobel Prize in Literature in 1957. He was killed in a car crash on 4 January 1960, at the age of 46.

Camus is junior by twelve years to André Malraux and by eight years to Jean-Paul Sartre. All three are university trained intellectuals, all three are creative writers whose works have enlightened their times, all three are lucid, passionate, articulate and deeply involved in the issues of the age, although their solutions are different. Camus had no doubts as to the value of literature and the vital rôle of the writer; he saw no difficulty in pursuing his journalism at the same time as his literary work, considering both to be equally relevant. This is what he said in a radio interview in 1953:

L'une des tentations de l'artiste est de se croire solidaire et il arrive en vérité qu'on le lui crie avec une assez ignoble joie. Mais il n'en est rien. Il se tient au milieu de tous, au niveau exact, ni plus haut ni plus bas, de tous ceux qui travaillent et qui luttent. Sa vocation même, devant l'oppression, est d'ouvrir les prisons et de faire parler le malheur et le bonheur de tous. C'est ici que l'art, contre ses ennemis, se justifie en faisant éclater justement qu'il n'est, lui, l'ennemi de personne. A lui seul, il ne saurait sans doute assurer la renaissance qui suppose justice et liberté. Mais sans lui, cette renaissance serait sans formes, et, partant, ne serait rien. Sans la culture, et la liberté relative qu'elle suppose, la société, même parfaite, n'est qu'une jungle. C'est pourquoi toute création authentique est un don à l'avenir.[3]

In this declaration, there is a denial of the Sartrian doctrine of *engagement*. As Eugène Ionesco has said, to be *engagé* is to lose one's liberty as a writer since he then becomes engaged in a battle for *one* ideology against another. Camus said firmly in 1948 before an international audience of writers that the writer cannot be 'complice de ceux qui emploient le langage ou les moyens des idéologies contemporaines'. It is vain and derisory, he said, to demand of the writer *justification* and *engagement* to a narrow dogma; he lives in his age and his duty is other:

C'est au nom de la passion de l'homme pour ce qu'il y a d'unique en l'homme, que nous refuserons toujours ces entreprises qui se couvrent de ce qu'il y a de plus misérable dans la raison.[4]

53

The denial of ideologies, those convenient crutches for those who do not wish to think for themselves, is the hallmark of Camus's own thought. His transparent honesty, awkward and difficult as it is is, shines through his work.

III

The appearance of *L'Etranger* in 1942 disconcerted readers for, as Jean-Paul Sartre remarked, 'au milieu de la production littéraire du temps, ce roman était lui-même un étranger'.[5] The meaning of the novel became clearer a little later in the same year with the publication of *Le Mythe de Sisyphe*, a collection of essays which dealt with the problems of the absurd world. The volume bears as its epigraph a sentence from Pindar: 'O mon âme, n'aspire pas à la vie immortelle, mais épuise le champ du possible', which is also the epigraph of Paul Valéry's well-known poem *Le Cimetière marin*. However different these two writers may be, they share a common ambition expressed in Valéry's words as 'il faut tenter de vivre'. Meursault, the *étranger* of the novel, lives in Algiers, a *petit employé*, 'un homme pauvre et nu, amoureux du soleil qui ne laisse pas d'ombres', as Camus later described him.[6] Patently uninvolved in ambition, sentimental success or in close relations with others, he is, although the central character in a novel written in the first person, curiously taciturn. His most common reaction is 'ça m'est égal' and this indifference merges into confusion. The orderly, explicable universe common to the first person narrative (see, above all, Proust) is replaced by a description, rather than an analysis, of an incoherent world of doubt. Technically, this device is extremely successful for we, the readers, see the world as Meursault sees it, at first hand so to speak, without any deforming commentary; our experience of the absurd world is vividly fresh, it is not explained, but rather *is*. Meursault's killing of the Arab is involuntary and the words used to describe it are 'la gâchette a cédé', 'the trigger gave way': the action is a blind, muscular twitch brought about by the dazzle of the sun. This is distorted in the trial. So Meursault, whose most positive characteristic is described by Camus as moved by 'une passion profonde, parce que tenace, [. . .] la passion de l'absolu et de la vérité', finds himself on trial because, as the author remarks, with Voltairean irony, 'dans notre société tout homme qui ne pleure pas à l'enterrement de sa mère risque d'être condamné à mort'. Meursault is 'le seul christ que nous méritions'.

What then is the experience of absurdity? It is born of man's existence in the world and has many constituent elements. There is the brevity of man's life and the swift passing of time (a theme common to poets from Horace onwards); the alien quality and hostility of the world with its

54

resultant alienation; the divorce in man between mind and body; the mechanical nature of the work imposed on men by their jobs in an industrial society; the fundamental isolation of one man from another caused by the difficulty of communication; the rôle of chance and, above all, the variety of truths in whose abstract name acts of cruelty and violence are committed. This diagnosis is by no means original to Camus; the climate of the absurd world is also that of the novels of Malraux and Sartre, who sees its origins as dating from the seventeenth century, quoting Pascal's definition of 'le malheur naturel de notre condition faible et mortelle et si misérable que rien ne peut nous consoler, lorsque nous y pensons de près'.[7] For the Christian there can be the saving grace of God but what happens to man when God is dead, for there is then no absolute authority for the traditional distinction between good and evil, right and wrong? Conflicting political ideologies countenance injustice in the name of abstractions. The myth of the glory of war is exploded to reveal its horror; the face of justice can disguise legal murder (Camus was bitterly opposed to capital punishment). If God is dead, man cannot transcend himself in His service; where then is the possibility of man achieving saintliness? Life has not an established meaning but is a chaos on which each man must seek to establish his own order; the experience of living involves *angoisse* and is commonly described in images of prison, siege, exile and quarantine.

Le Mythe de Sisyphe begins with this uncompromising sentence: 'Il n'y a qu'un problème philosophique vraiment sérieux: c'est le suicide. Juger que la vie vaut ou ne vaut pas la peine d'être vécue, c'est répondre à la question fondamentale de la philosophie'. It is to this question that the figure of Sisyphus provides an answer. Condemned by the gods throughout eternity to roll a stone up a hill only to see it roll down again when the summit has been attained so that he is endlessly compelled to recommence his pointless task, he is the archetypal figure of man in an absurd situation, a situation from which suicide might be seen to be the only escape. But, even in the face of this cruel and pointless torment, Camus observes that Sisyphus, because he understands the absurdity of his absurd task and its essential hopelessness, rises superior to it. The most dreadful truths can lose their awful power when once we have accepted them; so, concludes Camus, 'il faut imaginer Sisyphe heureux'. Camus expressed his hope in a clear and less allegorical way in 1944, when, in his *Lettres à un ami allemand*, he argued that the Germans had chosen the path of injustice, in the way of the gods, but that there was another way:

J'ai choisi la justice au contraire, pour rester fidèle à la terre. Je continue à croire que ce monde n'a pas de sens supérieur. Mais je sais que quelque chose en lui a du

55

sens et c'est l'homme, parce qu'il est le seul être à exiger d'en avoir. Ce monde a du moins la vérité de l'homme et notre tâche est de lui donner ses raisons contre le destin lui-même. Et il n'a pas d'autre raisons que l'homme et c'est celui-ci qu'il faut sauver si l'on veut sauver l'idée qu'on se fait de la vie. Votre sourire et votre dédain me diront: qu'est-ce sauver l'homme? Mais je vous le crie de tout moi-même, c'est ne pas le mutiler et c'est donner ses chances à la justice qu'il est le seul à concevoir.[8]

L'Etranger is required reading if one is to extract the full flavour and value from *La Peste*; Camus himself said that there was a progression from one work to the other. If suicide is not a solution, then it can only be by revolt that man can succeed in imposing his own order on the world. *La Peste* describes revolt in action, the collection of essays *L'Homme révolté* (1951) examines the history and principles of revolt. 'L'homme révolté,' says Camus, 'est un homme qui dit non'. He refuses injustice and cruelty but accepts that there is a better order for which it is right to fight. This is not egotistical, indeed, above all, it is a movement of solidarity:

La solidarité des hommes se fonde sur le mouvement de révolte et celui-ci, à son tour, ne trouve de justification que dans cette complicité. Nous serons donc en droit de dire que toute révolte qui s'autorise à nier ou à détruire cette solidarité perd du même coup le nom de révolte et coïncide en réalité avec un consentement meurtrier. De même cette solidarité, hors du sacré, ne prend vie qu'au niveau de la révolte. Le vrai drame de la pensée révoltée est alors annoncé. Pour être, l'homme doit se révolter; mais sa révolte doit respecter la limite qu'elle découvre en elle-même et où les hommes, en se rejoignant, commencent d'être.[9]

When man recognizes the absurdity and apparent sterility of the world, he suffers individually because the experience of the absurd is personal and solitary, but from the first single movement of revolt against this condition, revolt becomes collective, 'elle est l'aventure de tous'. To recognize that all men are prey to this same suffering is in itself a progress. Camus argues that 'le mal qui éprouvait un seul homme devient peste collective' and concludes, in a new Cartesian formula, 'je me révolte, donc nous sommes'.

IV

Incidents, characters and themes of what will become *La Peste* are noted in Camus's notebooks from 1938 onwards in a slow maturation and evolution; in an appendix to the Pléiade edition of his works (the volume entitled *Théâtre, Récits, Nouvelles*) may be read fascinating extracts from earlier states of the novel. In 1938, there are notes on Jeanne, the absent wife of Grand. In September 1939, the outbreak of war caused Camus to write 'la guerre apprend à tout perdre'; here is the germ of analogies between the destructive effects of war and those of the plague. In Oran, in 1941, he comes across the old man who spits on cats and notes, for the first time, a possible title: *La Peste ou Aventure (roman)*. In October of that year he begins to read around plagues in general and to document himself thoroughly on their historical and medical aspects. Then his mind turns to problems of literary structure and he reads Daniel Defoe's *Journal of the Plague Year* (1722) and Herman Melville's *Moby Dick* (1851) in which the whale becomes a symbol of man's quest and obsession. The epigraph of *La Peste* ('Il est aussi raisonnable de représenter une espèce d'emprisonnement par une autre que de représenter n'importe quelle chose qui existe réellement par quelquechose qui n'existe pas') is taken from Defoe; the handling of the symbolic structures in *Moby Dick* had a considerable influence. In 1942, there appear in the *Carnets* brief sketches of Cottard and *le vieil asthmatique*. At grips with the writing, he grapples with the figure of Tarrou: 'Qu'est-ce que je médite de plus grand que moi et que j'éprouve sans pouvoir le définir; une sorte de marche difficile vers une sainteté de la négation—héroïsme sans Dieu—l'homme pur enfin'.[10] He wonders whether to call the book *Les Prisonniers* but it is becoming clear in his mind that what he is writing will represent a progression in his attempted solution to the problems of which *L'Etranger* was *le point zéro*. At this stage, thoughts of the implications of the Occupation of France are uppermost in his mind and gradually the book begins to take on the shape of a tentative answer to the questions posed in *Le Mythe de Sisyphe*: what attitudes can man take in the face of the absurd world, how can man fight evil without employing evil methods? Camus finally settles on the theme of plague as the example of *maladie collective*. He rejects the Christian justification of suffering and notes in his *Carnets* in 1943: 'Ce que je reproche au christianisme, c'est qu'il est une doctrine d'injustice', a view which is to be developed in the first sermon of Paneloux. So, slowly, Camus accumulates notes, reflections and plans which shape the novel. More and more, the problem which presents itself is defined:

> Je ne suis pas un philosophe. Je ne crois pas assez à la raison pour croire à un système. Ce qui m'intéresse, c'est de savoir comment on peut se conduire quand on ne croit ni en Dieu ni en la raison.[11]

The different characters take on flesh and blood, reflecting different answers to the problem so sharply posed. A first version was finished in January 1943. It is not possible in this space to detail all the changes made between this version and the final published novel. There are changes in characters, Grand and Rambert do not exist, Cottard is a less complicated person; the movement of the novel is more hesitant; greater use is made of Rieux's notes. Camus was always greatly interested in language; the stylistic changes are great and achieved with difficulty. He suppresses any tendency to lyricism and strives to reinforce by the style, the idea that the novel is a *relation*, a *chronique*. He uses the *style indirect libre* as much as possible to emphasize the effect of monotony and, by contrast, to heighten the horror of death in the plague. The first person narrative of *L'Etranger* is here replaced by a narrator—whose identity is not revealed until late in the novel—speaking in the third person. The place of love is reduced and Camus adjures himself to 'faire de la séparation le grand thème du roman', to operate through the characters. He had arrived at the final form of the concept in which the plague had achieved the status of myth:

> Je veux exprimer au moyen de *La Peste* l'étouffement où nous avons tous souffert et l'atmosphère de menace et d'exil où nous avons vécu. Je veux du même coup étendre cette interprétation à la notion d'existence en général. Elle donnera l'image de ceux qui dans cette guerre ont eu la part de la réflexion et de la souffrance silencieuse et *morale*.[12]

V

In its published form, *La Peste* has achieved a stripped and sober form with an austere line. The Aristotelian doctrine of unity of action has considerable advantages for the writer since it permits him to achieve a pure line of development, stark yet profound. The five parts of the novel may be thought to correspond to the five acts of classical tragedy, tracing the beginnings, the development and the end of the plague. It is a *natural* plot, which reinforces the impression that this is documentary rather than fiction. Thus the first part describes the town of Oran and its inhabitants, with the beginnings of the plague which most wish to ignore. This section, which is in parts observed with considerable irony, ends with the recognition of the plague and the closing of the town, So isolation, separation, imprisonment are reinforced as a major theme of the novel whilst, at the same time, providing a unity of place in which the characters can move and meet each other with total naturalness. Technically, it performs the same function as the Maison Vauquer in Balzac's novel *Le Père Goriot*. As the ebb and flow of the plague progresses, the actions of the characters develop, caught as they are in the tensions of private self-interest and public good. The novel ends with the conquering of the plague, the end of imprisonment, amidst the 'cris d'allégresse' which echo through the town, but its last sentence contains a warning. Rieux, in his final reflection, remembers that 'le bacille de la peste ne meurt ni ne disparaît jamais'; the novel is open-ended, for 'la peste' still threatens us all. Perhaps here Camus is fulfilling the ambition once voiced by André Gide, to write a novel which would, at its end, bear the words 'POURRAIT ÊTRE CONTINUÉ' rather than 'FIN'.

The epigraph from Defoe encourages us to understand that the novel conceals more than one meaning. In Baudelaire's poem *Le Cygne* the status of the swan as symbol unfolds gradually with growing conviction as the poem progresses. The length of a novel denies the possibility of compression presented by a short poem and Camus has correctly judged it wise to warn the reader at once of the symbolic nature of the plague, of the reflections on the human dilemma which the narrative will arouse. On the surface, then, the novel may be read as a straightforward, gripping chronicle of the effects of the plague on a small town and as a description of the reactions of different characters to the horrors of imminent death. At this level, it is essential that the novel should move quickly. On another level, although the novel was in Camus's mind before the beginning of the war, it contains a number of pertinent observations on the German occupation of France during the war, or, more generally, on the moral and physical state of any conquered country. Rationing, electricity cuts, camps, repressive measures and the black market are all part of the administrative fight against the plague but it is also a faithful description of the Occupation of France, of which Camus had first-hand experience. On the third level, the plague represents the evil inherent in the human condition, the cruelty of the absurd world. It reveals the possible reactions of man in such a situation and reflects on the nature of human revolt against inhumanity and on the moral issues involved. The imprisonment is physical but separation and exile are seen as part of man's destiny, just as they are in Baudelaire's *Le Cygne*. Professor Cruickshank has justly observed that, in *La Peste*:

> the three major areas of human experience are included—the personal, the social, the speculative—and all three are unified in the symbol of the plague. In this way Camus attempts, through his novel, to make contact with the whole experience of man, with the triple living and thinking of the reader.[13]

The use of the symbol in literature had been widely practised and discussed from Baudelaire onwards; the desire to make a work of literature suggest, rather than affirm, to make its harmonics echo after the printed page had been closed was and still is an ambition present in the mind of many writers. But if a symbol is to work, it must be totally consistent at all levels and consistent *between* each level. From this point of view, *La Peste* is literary *tour de force*.

Reference has already been made to the form of narrative employed by Camus: the anonymous narrator using the third person and favouring the *style indirect*. Yet the narrator is present at all the main events as an observer and participant. He could have spoken in the first person but

Camus ascribes to him the third person for a number of reasons. The narrator has direct knowledge of the events and so can enlighten the reader with economical directness; he retains a certain objectivity; his very anonymity frees us of the urge to wonder why *Rieux* (for the narrator is revealed to be he) says this or does that. He is depersonalized. Above all, it presents a certain distance between us and the appalling events which might threaten to overwhelm the reader. Here Camus is walking a tightrope. The first quality of a novel must be its readability, for if it is not read, it is nothing. The power to grip us and to involve us in the fictional world created by the author is paramount. It is a gift which the Spanish philosopher Ortega y Gasset described as 'impermeability', the gift vested in a great novelist to turn us into citizens of Paris in 1819 (as in Balzac's *Le Père Goriot*) or of Moscow (as in Tolstoy's *Anna Karenina*), to abstract us from our own personal and temporal difficulties as citizens of another country at another time. But Camus is not a simple story-teller; he is dramatizing a moral position which he considers to be central to his age and if the reader does not become totally involved with the fate of the characters, he will not be encouraged to continue his meditation on his personal concern with the moral issues. If revolt is collective, then it must spread out from the pages of the novel to the real towns and the real lives of real readers. This is a technical problem which Camus solves with great success. However, the problem remains that the plague is not self-inflicted but strikes haphazardly and blindly; it is not deliberately chosen by any human agency as war and political violence are chosen; it lies beyond any human responsibility.

La Peste then is, above all, a study of men striving in suffering against the problem of evil. It is a fact they are slow to recognize and reluctant to accept. This is made clear by the unwillingness of the town to admit the plague for what it is; the *concierge*, at the very beginning of the novel, is typical of this refusal. The administration takes refuge in empty formulas, they set up a committee (*P*. p.1,227; *M*. p.25).[14] Men cling to the most fragile of straws and become irrational, pathetic victims of hope (*P*. p.1,232; *M*. p.32). The growing helplessness of men who are not equipped to deal with this major disaster and prefer to bury their heads in the sand like ostriches is faithfully reflected in the unemotional, documentary style of a report. Richard, the senior doctor, argues that all he can do is to speak to the Préfet. The Press is irresponsible but events gain momentum until finally the dreadful name of the plague is pronounced. At this point, the moralist in Camus takes over (see *P*. pp.1,245–6; *M*. pp.49–53). Man is engaged in a search for happiness which is a laudable end in itself in

Camus's view, but happiness is not to be attained when evil is abroad; man lives in illusion if he believes otherwise. He may believe himself to be free but freedom for the individual is illusory as long as evil—'cette énormité'—exists. By the end of the first section, hope is swept aside, the town is closed, the dreadful effects of isolation and evil are abroad. It is at this point that solidarity begins to be glimpsed as the only solution for 'à partir de ce moment, il est possible de dire que la peste fut notre affaire à nous tous' (*P.* p 1,271; *M* p 81) The rest of the novel works out the implications of the collective realization of evil, individual reactions to it and the attempts to understand the morality behind it. Images of exile and imprisonment multiply, with their opposites, windows and blue skies. The citizens begin to act, says the narrator, 'comme s'ils n'avaient pas de sentiments individuels' (*P.* p.1,271; *M.* p.82). In the face of death, pity is not enough since, says the narrator, 'on se fatigue de la pitié quand la pitié est inutile' (*P.* p.1,290; *M.* p.106). But the effect of the plague is so overwhelming that it leads to a kind of 'consentement provisoire', to the suppression of 'jugements de valeur'. We must understand by this that evil destroys humanity, is contagious and insidious because it inhibits the search for solutions: 'l'habitude du désespoir est pire que le désespoir lui-même' (*P.* p.1,364; *M.* p.200).

Why has Oran been singled out for this trial? If this problem could be solved, something might be learned of the nature of evil. There is clearly an explanation in terms of punishment for sin which can be advanced by the Christian church. This is introduced by Camus with one of those ironic notes in which *La Peste* abounds ('les autorités ecclésiastiques de notre ville décidèrent de lutter contre la peste par leurs propres moyens, en organisant une semaine de prières collectives' *P.* p.1,292; *M.* p.107). The first sermon preached by the militant Jesuit, Père Paneloux, begins with 'une seule phrase véhémente et martelée: "Mes frères, vous êtes dans le malheur, mes frères, vous l'avez mérité" ' (*P.* p.1,294; *M.* p.110). The change of personal pronoun is charged with significance. The form of address 'mes frères' is the traditional form used by priest to parishioner, the bite is in the use of the second person plural, '*vous* êtes dans le malheur . . ., *vous* l'avez mérité'. This brutal disassociation of the priest from the people argues that the people have abused the charity of God and the town is now 'privé de la lumière de Dieu'. Not all Christians would accept this idea of a savage retribution and for the non-believer like Camus, for the *révoltés*, there is something totally unacceptable in the spectacle of men, women and children being indiscriminately sentenced for an unknown crime. In this situation, the *révolté* says 'No': 'quand on voit la misère et la douleur qu'elle apporte, il faut être fou, aveugle ou

61

lâche pour se résigner à la peste' (*P.* p.1,320; *M.* p.142). The second sermon preached by Père Paneloux comes soon after the horrible death from the plague of the young son of Othon, the examining magistrate, at which both he and Rieux had been present. Rieux says to Paneloux with unconcealed bitterness: 'Ah! celui-là, au moins, était innocent, vous le savez bien!' (*P.* p.1,394; *M.* p.237). Paneloux expresses his view that the measure of suffering exceeds our understanding and so 'devons-nous aimer ce que nous ne pouvons pas comprendre' but Rieux, in this conflict between religion and science, brushes aside this reasoning, saying: 'Non, mon père. Je me fais une autre idée de l'amour. Et je refuserai jusqu'à la mort d'aimer cette création où des enfants sont torturés'. To compare the two sermons in detail is to reveal the shock which the plague has administered to the priest. The delivery, which, in the first sermon, was strong and emphatic, is now considerably more hesitant and, 'chose curieuse encore, il ne disait plus "vous", mais "nous"' (*P.* p.1,399; *M.* p.243). The movement of identification is complete and in the end Paneloux has to argue that the acceptance of suffering involves the ultimate acceptance of faith. His death soon afterwards is ambiguous. Did he die of the plague or not? Are his real torments physical or are they inspired by a profound and racking crisis of faith? The verdict on his death as a 'cas douteux' refers to more than any medical diagnosis.

VI

The austerity of plot of *La Peste* means that the richness of the novel lies in the characters and their interactions. Thoughtful and implacably lucid, they embody a variety of possible attitudes in the face of the plague. They are not presented in Balzacian detail; all we know about their life before the plague is limited to the little we need to know to understand their present attitudes: Cottard's crime, Grand's missing wife, Tarrou's experience of official justice. Their physical attributes, financial or social status, are absent. They bear a resemblance to the characters of André Gide, having suffered that 'erosion of contours' which he quotes with approval. This slight stylization gives us a certain emotional distance and invites independent judgment. It is not that they are not human but that in addition to their humanity, they also live in a moral dimension.

RIEUX, the narrator, is in a special situation in the plague. As a doctor he is bound by the Hippocratic Oath to fight illness and suffering. He has no choice of action and so his motives are straightforward and unambiguous. This puts him into an ideal position as a narrator in addition to his medical objectivity. His tendency towards moral discrimination allows him to make the transition from the plague as fact to the plague as symbol. Rieux strikes no heroic stances adopting rather the simple, consistent attitude of refusing injustice and concessions. In a discussion with Tarrou (*P.* p.1,321; *M.* pp.144 *et seq.*) he describes his own ambition as being a fight against death; to Paneloux, he rejects salvation which is too big a word for him. Towards the end of the novel, he makes clear his central belief:

> Je me sens plus de solidarité avec les vaincus qu'avec les saints. Je n'ai pas de goût, je crois, pour l'héroïsme et la sainteté. Ce qui m'intéresse, c'est d'être un homme (*P.* p.1,425; *M.* p.276)

In many ways, Rieux is the spokesman of many of Camus's own attitudes —the protest against the unintelligibility of a cruel world and its suffering, the deep compassion and respect for man, the distrust of abstractions like salvation, saintliness, heroism, the creative drive of revolt.

Yet, Rieux uses the word 'héros' to describe GRAND, 'ce héros insignifiant et effacé qui n'avait pour lui qu'un peu de bonté au coeur et un idéal apparemment ridicule' (*P.* p.1,329; *M.* p.154). He is not of the stuff of the traditional hero—his solitude, his pathetic search for the perfect sentence, his absurd efforts in the field of stylistics, his withdrawn nature ('heureusement j'ai mon travail,' he says at the beginning of the novel), present him as an introspective eccentric. When the fury of the plague strikes the town, his actions are simple, instinctive and good. He fights in the only way he can, administratively and statistically. Grand is an innocent who represents Camus's faith in human goodness. Like Dr Rieux, Grand serves his fellow men without seeking to erect great metaphysical theories; there is no aspiration towards any absolutes. There is a certain sentimentality in his presentation as in the Christmas scene before the shop window when he recalls his lost love. At the end of the trials of the plague, Grand is burning to begin his life work again and has restarted his sentence by omitting all the adjectives. One would be tempted to describe him as the average man if such a phrase had any meaning.

TARROU, the intellectual, is the counterpart of Grand. Both arrive at the same devoted, self-sacrificing service against evil but in different ways. Both catch the plague and Tarrou dies of it, ironically almost the last recorded case. Whilst Grand's actions are instinctive and therefore non-thinking, Tarrou worries to find an intellectual justification for his acts and to build a morality. Tarrou, who is much drawn to Rieux, confesses that he had left home at the age of seventeen, when he had heard his father, whom he had much admired until then, demand the death penalty for an accused man: here the character echoes Camus's own hatred of capital punishment. Tarrou then took part in various political movements devoted to the fight for justice but discovered that these very actions led to further cruelty and violence:

> J'ai compris alors que moi, du moins, je n'avais pas cessé d'être un pestiféré pendant toutes ces longues années où pourtant, de toute mon âme, je croyais lutter justement contre la peste. J'ai appris que j'avais indirectement souscrit à la mort de milliers d'hommes, que j'avais même provoqué cette mort en trouvant bons les actions et les principes qui l'avaient fatalement entraînée (*P.* p.1,422; *M.* p.272).

Now in Oran, he is in a moral crisis, trying to purge himself of guilt, to transcend himself by his own means. In the character of Tarrou, the symbolic side of the plague is very clear for he confesses that 'je souffrais déjà de la peste bien avant de connaître cette ville'. It is Tarrou who poses the question which is perhaps central to the novel and to Camus's own thought:

> Peut-on être un saint sans Dieu, c'est le seul problème concret que je connaisse aujourd'hui (*P.* p.1,425; *M.* p.276).

Yet his action in the organization of the 'cordons sanitaires' eventually cost him his life and so answered his own question.

RAMBERT is the hedonist seeking the personal pleasure he considers to be man's due. Caught in Oran, he is desperately conscious of the passing of time and of the fragile nature of happiness which he considers to be found above all in love. In the early stages of the novel, he constantly reminds Dr Rieux 'qu'il n'avait pas de rapport avec Oran, que ce n'était pas son affaire d'y rester, qu'il se trouvait là par accident' (*P.* p.1,286; *M.* p.99) and he makes reckless attempts to escape from the prison of the town. He is so involved in his personal search that 'les progrès de la peste lui échappaient pratiquement' and yet his doubts begin; he begins to defend himself vigorously although he is never attacked. He is not a coward, he says, but 'je ne crois pas à l'héroïsme', rather 'ce qui m'intéresse, c'est qu'on vive et qu'on meure de ce qu'on aime' (*P.* p.1,349; *M.* p.179). An increasing guilt grips him and in this same dialogue in which Rieux, steadfastly refusing rhetoric and heroism, declares that 'la seule façon de lutter contre la peste, c'est l'honnêteté', Rambert angrily replies 'peut-être en effet suis-je dans mon tort en choisissant l'amour'. At the moment when all his efforts to escape appear to be crowned with success, he renounces his plans and throws in his lot with Rieux: 'il peut y avoir de la honte à être heureux tout seul'. This dramatic change is perhaps not coherently argued but it is nonetheless an example of the conscience in action and the sweeping power of solidarity in revolt against evil.

COTTARD is in a different category. Wanted by the police, he was an outsider, exiled from society, before the plague began. He is a lonely man who has cast himself in the rôle of exploiter of others. Cottard feels a certain relief when the plague makes *étrangers* of all men since it seems to him to be an extension of the moral climate in which he lived. Tarrou understands this rather incoherent man who grows in stature and good humour. Here is Tarrou's comment on Cottard:

> Il est menacé comme les autres, mais justement, il l'est avec les autres. Et ensuite, il ne pense pas sérieusement, j'en suis sûr, qu'il puisse être atteint par la peste. Il a l'air de vivre sur cette idée, pas si bête d'ailleurs, qu'un homme en proie à une grande maladie, ou à une angoisse profonde, est dispensé du même coup de toutes les autres maladies ou angoisses (*P.* p.1,376; *M.* p.213).

The alienated man is at home in a world where alienation becomes the climate in which all must live.

These characters, together with the figure of Paneloux whom I have already discussed and the minor personages, form part of the rich and complex tapestry which is *La Peste*. It is a picture of some of the great issues of the twentieth century and from this great ambition grow the themes. There is the theme of evil and man's reaction to it; the theme of the collective action of revolt to conquer evil; separation and exile as part of the human condition; solitude and suffering; man's obstinate search for happiness and his unquenchable hope. This accords with Camus's own conception of the aim of the novel in general:

> La vraie création romanesque . . . utilise le réel et n'utilise que lui, avec sa chaleur et son sang, ses passions ou ses cris. Simplement, elle y ajoute quelque chose qui le transfigure.[15]

This 'quelque chose qui le transfigure' Camus has in abundance for he is a writer who is as conscious as Baudelaire of the convincing power of literary effects. Living as he did at a time when art itself is in revolt against tradition and convention, Camus never lost sight of the fact that art needs to *communicate* with men and women. In an interview held only a fortnight or so before his death, Camus was asked whether he agreed with a generally held view of critics that the novel was dying. This was his answer:

> L'erreur de l'art moderne est presque toujours de faire passer le moyen avant la fin, la forme avant le fond, la technique avant le sujet. Si les techniques d'art me passionnent et si je cherche à les posséder toutes c'est que je veux pouvoir m'en servir librement, les réduire au rang d'outils.[16]

For Camus, the novel is another weapon in the fight for justice and charity.

65

NOTES

References to the works of Albert Camus are taken from: Camus, *Théâtre, Récits, Nouvelles, préface par* Jean Grenier, *textes établis et annotés par* Roger Quilliot, 1962 and *Essais, introduction par* R. Quilliot, *textes établis et annotés par* R. Quilliot *et* L. Faucon, 1965, both published in Paris by the Bibliothèque de la Pléiade. Page references to the text of *La Peste* are also given from: Albert Camus, *La Peste*, ed. W. J. Strachan, London, Methuen, 1962.

1 'Lettres sur la révolte', *Essais*, p.743.
2 J. Cruickshank, *Albert Camus and the Literature of Revolt*, Oxford University Press, 1959. Page references are to the 1970 edition. [This is essential reading.]
3 'L'artiste et son temps', *Essais*, p.804.
4 'Le témoin de la liberté', *ibid.*, p.405.
5 'Explication de *L'Etranger*', *Situations*, 1, Paris, Gallimard, 1947, p.99.
6 In a preface dated 8 January 1955 to an American edition, *Théâtre, Récits, Nouvelles*, p.1,920.
7 *Situations, i*, p.101.
8 *Essais*, p.241.
9 *L'Homme révolté*, *Essais*, p.431.
10 *Théâtre, Récits, Nouvelles*, p.1,928.
11 Interview of 1945, *Essais*, p.1,427.
12 *Théâtre, Récits, Nouvelles*, p.1,934.
13 *Op. cit.*, p.172. The chapter on 'The Art of the Novel (II)' contains a valuable discussion of this and other similar questions.
14 To facilitate the use of page references, I have given the page numbers of two editions of *La Peste*: the Pléiade edition in *Théâtre, Récits, Nouvelles* (abbreviated to *P*) and the edition prepared by W. J. Strachan, London, Methuen (abbreviated to *M*).
15 *L'Homme révolté*, *Essais*, p.673.
16 Interview of 20 December 1959, *Essais*, p.1,927.

SUMMARY BIBLIOGRAPHY

BRÉE, GERMAINE, *Camus*, New Brunswick, Rutgers University Press, 1961.
CRUICKSHANK, JOHN, *Albert Camus and the Literature of Revolt*, London and New York, Oxford University Press, 1959.
CRUICKSHANK, JOHN, (ed.), *The Novelist as Philosopher, Studies in French Fiction 1935–1960*, London, Oxford University Press, 1962.
FITCH, B. T., *Le Sentiment d'étrangeté chez Malraux, Sartre, Camus et Simone de Beauvoir*, Paris, Minard, 1964.
GINESTIER, PAUL, *Pour connaître la pensée de Camus*, Paris, Bordas, 1964.
HAGGIS, D. R., *La Peste*, London, Arnold.
LEBESGUE, M., *Camus par lui-même*, Paris, Ed. du Seuil, 1963.
LÉVI-VALENSI, J., (ed.), *Les Critiques de notre temps et Camus*, Paris, Garnier, 1970.
RHEIN, P. H., *Albert Camus*, New York, Twayne, 1969.
SCOTT, NATHAN A., *Camus*, London, Bowes and Bowes, 1962.
THODY, PHILIP, *Albert Camus: A Study of his Work*, London, Hamish Hamilton, 1957.
ULLMANN, STEPHEN, *The Image in the Modern French Novel*, Cambridge University Press, 1960. (See particularly Chap.IV 'The two styles of Camus').

La Peste. Commentary

'Les curieux événements qui font le sujet de cette chronique . . .
il soit impossible d'apercevoir la mer qu'il faut toujours aller
chercher' (*P.* pp.1,217–9; *M.* pp.13–16).

1   Les curieux événements qui font le sujet de cette chronique se
sont produits en 194., à Oran. De l'avis général, ils n'y étaient
pas à leur place, sortant un peu de l'ordinaire. A première vue,
Oran est, en effet, une ville ordinaire et rien de plus qu'une
préfecture française de la côte algérienne.

2   La cité elle-même, on doit l'avouer, est laide. D'aspect
tranquille, il faut quelque temps pour apercevoir ce qui la rend
différente de tant d'autres villes commerçantes sous toutes les
latitudes. Comment faire imaginer par exemple, une ville sans
pigeons, sans arbres et sans jardins, où l'on ne rencontre ni
battements d'ailes ni froissements de feuilles, un lieu neutre
pour tout dire? Le changement des saisons ne s'y lit que dans
le ciel. Le printemps s'annonce seulement par la qualité de
l'air ou par les corbeilles de fleurs que des petits vendeurs
ramènent des banlieues; c'est un printemps qu'on vend sur les
marchés. Pendant l'été, le soleil incendie les maisons trop sèches
et couvre les murs d'une cendre grise; on ne peut plus vivre
alors que dans l'ombre des volets clos. En automne, c'est, au
contraire, un déluge de boue. Les beaux jours viennent seulement en hiver.

3   Une manière commode de faire la connaissance d'une ville
est de chercher comment on y travaille, comment on y aime et
comment on y meurt. Dans notre petite ville, est-ce l'effet du
climat, tout cela se fait ensemble, du même air frénétique et
absent. C'est-à-dire qu'on s'y ennuie et qu'on s'y applique à
prendre des habitudes. Nos concitoyens travaillent beaucoup,
mais toujours pour s'enrichir. Ils s'intéressent surtout au
commerce et ils s'occupent d'abord, selon leur expression, de
faire des affaires. Naturellement, ils ont du goût aussi pour les
joies simples, ils aiment les femmes, le cinéma et les bains de
mer. Mais, très raisonnablement, ils réservent ces plaisirs pour

le samedi soir et le dimanche, essayant, les autres jours de la semaine, de gagner beaucoup d'argent. Le soir, lorsqu'ils quittent leurs bureaux, ils se réunissent à heure fixe dans les cafés, ils se promènent sur le même boulevard ou bien ils se mettent à leurs balcons. Les désirs des plus jeunes sont violents et brefs, tandis que les vices des plus âgés ne dépassent pas les associations de boulomanes, les banquets des amicales et les cercles où l'on joue gros jeu sur le hasard des cartes.

4   On dira sans doute que cela n'est pas particulier à notre ville et qu'en somme tous nos contemporains sont ainsi. Sans doute, rien n'est plus naturel, aujourd'hui, que de voir des gens travailler du matin au soir et choisir ensuite de perdre aux cartes, au café, et en bavardages, le temps qui leur reste pour vivre. Mais il est des villes et des pays où les gens ont, de temps en temps, le soupçon d'autre chose. En général, cela ne change pas leur vie. Seulement, il y a eu le soupçon et c'est toujours cela de gagné. Oran, au contraire, est apparemment une ville sans soupçons, c'est-à-dire une ville tout à fait moderne. Il n'est pas nécessaire, en conséquence, de préciser la façon dont on s'aime chez nous. Les hommes et les femmes, ou bien se dévorent rapidement dans ce qu'on appelle l'acte d'amour, ou bien s'engagent dans une longue habitude à deux. Entre ces extrêmes, il n'y a pas souvent de milieu. Cela non plus n'est pas original. A Oran comme ailleurs, faute de temps et de réflexion, on est bien obligé de s'aimer sans le savoir.

5   Ce qui est plus original dans notre ville est la difficulté qu'on peut y trouver à mourir. Difficulté, d'ailleurs, n'est pas le bon mot et il serait plus juste de parler d'inconfort. Ce n'est jamais agréable d'être malade, mais il y a des villes et des pays qui vous soutiennent dans la maladie, où l'on peut, en quelque sorte, se laisser aller. Un malade a besoin de douceur il aime à s'appuyer sur quelque chose, c'est bien naturel. Mais à Oran, les excès du climat, l'importance des affaires qu'on y traite, l'insignifiance du décor, la rapidité du crépuscule et la qualité des plaisirs, tout demande la bonne santé. Un malade s'y trouve bien seul. Qu'on pense alors à celui qui va mourir, pris au piège derrière des centaines de murs crépitants de chaleur, pendant qu'à la même minute, toute une population, au téléphone ou dans les cafés, parle de traites, de connaissements

et d'escompte. On comprendra ce qu'il peut y avoir d'incon-
fortable dans la mort, même moderne, lorsqu'elle survient
ainsi dans un lieu sec.

6   Ces quelques indications donnent peut-être une idée suffisante
de notre cité. Au demeurant, on ne doit rien exagérer. Ce qu'il
fallait souligner, c'est l'aspect banal de la ville et de la vie.
Mais on passe ses journées sans difficultés aussitôt qu'on a des
habitudes. Du moment que notre ville favorise les habitudes,
on peut dire que tout est pour le mieux. Sous cet angle, sans
doute, la vie n'est pas très passionnante. Du moins, on ne
connaît pas chez nous le désordre. Et notre population franche,
sympathique et active, a toujours provoqué chez le voyageur
une estime raisonnable. Cette cité sans pittoresque, sans végétation et sans âme finit par sembler reposante, on s'y endort
enfin. Mais il est juste d'ajouter qu'elle s'est greffée sur un
paysage sans égal, au milieu d'un plateau nu, entouré de
collines lumineuses, devant une baie au dessin parfait. On
peut seulement regretter qu'elle se soit construite en tournant
le dos à cette baie et que, partant, il soit impossible d'apercevoir
la mer qu'il faut toujours aller chercher.

Introduction:

The passage chosen consists of the opening pages of *La Peste.* The first
paragraphs of a novel are privileged and carry a peculiar responsibility for
it is essential that they should persuade the casual reader that the book is
'worth reading'; they should also establish at once a tone which will
dominate the novel. It is not appropriate in a commentary to attempt long,
detailed comparisons with other novels but the extraordinarily daring
nature of Camus's opening paragraphs will only become apparent if it is
set beside the opening of other novels. Take, for example, the beginning of
Balzac's *Le Père Goriot.* The first words describe Mme Vauquer and her
pension; the time is 1819, 'époque où ce drame commence'. Balzac defends
his choice of the word 'drame' and already our attention is compromised
for we are being told that drama and tragedy lie in wait for us; we shall
read on with a different kind of emphasis. There follows a series of reflections on the Paris which is the setting of the novel, with a constant insistence on its special individuality; Balzac even goes so far as to doubt
whether the implications of the work will be understood by those who do
not know the city. This is to turn the reader into an uncommitted spectator:
unless he himself lives in this 'vallée remplie de souffrances réelles', he may

expect to avoid the horrors which are to be unfolded. Balzac himself seems to become conscious of this error for he hastily warns us:

> Ah! sachez-le: ce drama n'est ni une fiction, ni un roman. *All is true*, il est si véritable, que chacun peut en reconnaître les éléments chez soi, dans son coeur peut-être.

Here the author has intervened with all his authority to influence the way in which we shall follow the story, he has commanded the reader to a certain interpretation.

The opening paragraph of Zola's *Germinal* aims at a different effect. In three powerful sentences, the reader meets a solitary man walking through an immense plain in the complete darkness of night. Here the effect is obtained through the loaded emotive use of language. There is an insistence on the immensity of the distances, the 'plaine rase', 'la sensation de l'immense horizon plat', 'des rafales larges comme sur une mer'. Secondly, the lack of colour in the threatening blackness is emphasized in 'la nuit sans étoiles, d'une obscurité et d'une épaisseur d'encre', 'le sol noir', 'l'embrun aveuglant des ténèbres'. In this threatening landscape, the solitary figure of man is dwarfed by nature, his isolation accentuated by the menace around him, stated not in direct terms, but by the imaginative use of language. In this way the scene is set for the titanic struggle between the miners and the blind forces of the mine.

La Peste begins in a way which denies the effects achieved by Balzac and Zola. Oran is presented as Everytown and Rieux as Everyman. The language used is deliberately flat and unemotional.

General Character

The passage is descriptive and its purpose is to set the scene for what is to follow in the unprecedented events of the plague. It is precise in that the town of Oran exists, although it would not be personally known to most readers of the novel, and this adds a presumed authenticity. The date, 194–, is also given although it is deliberately not too precise in case it should be identified too closely with the North African campaigns. There is one very significant fact. The original version of the novel began with what is now the second subsection ('Le matin du 16 avril, le docteur Bernard Rieux sortit de son cabinet et buta sur un rat mort, au milieu du palier') and the description of Oran came with the second chapter. The discovery of the first dead rats provides a much more dramatic beginning. Why did Camus reverse the order? It is clear that the description of the town has a real importance but whilst Balzac tells us himself of the rare and untoward nature of the events we are about to witness and Zola

70

impresses us with a sense of brooding, impending fear, the Oran of Camus is different. Sunny, modern, almost featureless, it is absorbed in its commercial life. It is reassuringly ordinary.

Thought Structure

Paragraph 1 introduces the reader to Oran, described immediately as 'une ville ordinaire' and therefore an unexpected setting for the 'curieux événements' which are to follow. It is to be noted that the work is described as a 'chronique', a form which is not thought of as being predominantly literary in form or in intention.

Paragraph 2 describes the face of this ugly town. It is 'tranquille' but *neuter*; even its changing seasons are unremarkable.

Paragraph 3 suggests another way of looking at a town: 'comment on y travaille, comment on y aime et comment on y meurt'. These are three basic human activities and all three will be particularly affected by the plague. This paragraph discusses the habit of work, obsessive but 'toujours pour s'enrichir'. The picture of a materialistic town begins to emerge in which passions are modest and habits strong. The description insists on boredom and habit as a defence against the unknown. We shall see that habit is not strong enough to withstand the plague, however comforting routine may be.

Paragraph 4 reveals that the act of love is either brief, 'les hommes et les femmes . . . se dévorent rapidement dans ce qu'on appelle l'acte d'amour', or becomes 'une longue habitude à deux'. The town is smug and has not the slightest 'soupçon d'autre chose'. It is self-sufficient and enclosed. Indeed, it is already a kind of moral prison, if not yet a physical one. One of the remarkable paradoxes which will emerge as the novel progresses is this: as the town becomes a physical prison, its inhabitants break down the walls of their moral confinement, their smugness and routine, materialistic life.

Paragraph 5 discusses the attitudes of the inhabitants of Oran to death. This is perhaps an unexpected inclusion although death will become the daily companion of the Oranais but, of course, the narrator will eventually be identified as Dr Rieux whose experience of attitudes to death is of long standing. Illness is not tolerated here, 'un malade s'y trouvait bien seul'. In this 'lieu sec', there is a singular absence of compassion and this modern city has a primitive lack of charity in illness. Here again the stress is on a kind of blind egotism in which habit and lack of thought bring cruelty through indifference. It is not a deliberate cruelty but rather a kind of unintelligent acceptance, a lack of questioning. This takes on considerable importance later in the novel.

Paragraph 6 combines into one the two portraits of the town, the physical and the moral. Lest we should think of the inhabitants as monsters, we are reminded that they are ordinary people, 'ce qu'il fallait souligner, c'est l'aspect banal de la ville et de la vie'. They are in no way evil; if life in the town is not very 'passionnante', it is also orderly and pleasant on a muted, uncritical level. It is so quiet that 'on s'y endort enfin'. It is a way of life which lacks solidarity and the spirit of revolt.

Literary Construction:

With the example of Balzac and Zola fresh in mind, the flat, unemotional style of the extract hits us with force. Camus was North African in his upbringing and we know from essays like those contained in *Noces*, how sensitive and direct is his reaction to sun and sea. Nothing lyrical is to be found in the description of these opening paragraphs except at the end of the sixth paragraph where there is reference to the 'paysage sans égal', the 'collines lumineuses', the 'baie au dessin parfait'. The inhabitants, sunk in a kind of moral torpor, do not see it and turn their back on the sea 'qu'il faut toujours aller chercher'.

Another striking fact about the style of the passage is the marked lack of images. That Camus is a writer whose style is studded with sharp images and whose thought is often concretized in imaginative figurative forms is clear from the novel. In these opening paragraphs, the chronicler refuses the resource to the image and sets down, almost as in an inventory, the characteristics of the town and its inhabitants. The few images there are seem unremarkable like the lovers 'qui se dévorent' or summarize aptly, with great economy, what has gone before, like the description of the town as a 'lieu neutre'; They reinforce the quiet relationship between the town which is 'reposante' and its inhabitants. The one image which stands out by its originality and its shock of horror is, significantly, that of the dying man '*pris au piège* derrière des centaines de murs crépitants de chaleur, pendant qu'à la même minute, toute une population, au téléphone ou dans les cafés, parle de traites, de connaissements et d'escompte'. Here is introduced almost casually the theme which will dominate the book—traps, prisons, solitude and anguish.

A third remarkable feature of the passage is the number of negatives which are used in the description of the town. It is a town 'sans pigeons, sans arbres et sans jardins, où l'on ne rencontre ni battements d'ailes ni froissements de feuilles'; 'le changement des saisons ne s'y lit que dans le ciel'; it is a town 'sans soupçons', marked by 'l'insignifiance du décor'; here 'la vie n'est pas très passionnante' so that 'cette cité sans pittoresque, sans végétation et sans âme finit par sembler reposante, on s'y endort enfin'. In this way is built up an atmosphere of refusal.

Lastly, one must note how often the narrator, without any recourse to figurative language, tells us bluntly that the town *is* ordinary, typical and 'sans âme'. From the outset, the town is described unambiguously as 'une ville ordinaire'. It is in no way a place in which original attitudes are appreciated; 'ce qu'il fallait souligner, c'est l'aspect banal de la ville et de la vie'.

Conclusion

It is difficult to complete a commentary on a passage taken from a novel because, unlike a single poem, it is not complete in itself and one has to look backwards or forwards to check its context. Nevertheless, from the text itself, certain ideas and impressions emerge clearly.

The description of the town and of its inhabitants stresses their ordinariness but it is a moral definition as well as a purely physical one. The passage contains a number of stylistic refusals, all of which add to the overwhelming impression of banality: there is no lyrical description of the scene to which we know Camus to be enormously attached; the landscape is not interpreted in human terms; there are no dramatic effects; the style chosen is that of a *chronique*.

The inhabitants are characterized as being self-satisfied, smug and uncritical. This egotism means that each is separated and exiled from his neighbour in a kind of moral indifference which will be smashed by the coming of the plague.

What importance do these privileged opening pages have in the remainder of the novel? To look at the town from the point of view of 'comment on y travaille, comment on y aime et comment on y meurt' permits the accumulation of the moral to the physical and so establishes a mode of thought which will persist throughout the novel. The banality of the town establishes its neutrality and so, in literary terms, facilitates the transference of levels of meaning from chronicle to occupation to the plague as a generalized symbol of evil. The moral stance of the inhabitants emerges as the opposite of that which is required by man in the face of evil; egocentricity rather than solidarity, acceptance rather than revolt. The unemotional style heightens the horror.

It may be an ususual opening to a novel but of its effectiveness there can be no doubt.

A View of Twentieth-century French Literature

It is no more than a platitude to say that literature is concerned with the ordered portrayal of men and women in their relationships with each other. These relationships do not take place in a vacuum and even in plays as deeply concerned with the analysis of human attitudes as those of Racine, the presence of the outside world is deeply felt. His characters measure their individual passions and needs against the ethical and moral code of the society in which they live. Because society has a theoretical view of the way in which kings and queens should conduct themselves, Phèdre finds herself trapped between the irresistible force of her own passion and a moral standard imposed upon her because she *is* a queen. It is true that Racine's view of society is abstract and stable, containing no economic stresses, no political struggles. The movement of political ideas in the eighteenth century destroyed for ever the idea of a stable society and created the ferment of the nineteenth century in which social, political and economic pressures are seen as forces which moved human destiny. In literature, the 'democratization of tragedy', as it has been called, discovered a whole new range of tragic heroes: *vermicelliers*, like Balzac's Goriot; clerks, like Stendhal's Julien Sorel; doctors' wives, like Emma Bovary; miners, railway men, shop assistants, as in Zola. Balzac's characters, like their author, are enmeshed in a desperate struggle to achieve social status or simply to keep alive. The growth of an industrial society allows movement between the classes and fosters the importance of economic conditions. The portrayal of man in literature reflects this change; the novel becomes the chosen form for the great literary phenomenon of the nineteenth century is its rise to a position of pre-eminence. The novel, which had been born without the privilege of a long, classical heritage like tragedy or the epic poem, had been considered as an essentially unserious literary form, far down in the hierarchy of artistic values. Balzac had seen this very clearly and his famous *avant-propos* to the 1842 edition of *La Comédie humaine* contained the first spirited defence of the novel form. The novel can be, argued Balzac, as serious a witness to an age as philosophy or history. As a picture of society it can present an accurate analysis from which moral conclusions may be drawn; the novelist is indeed the 'instituteur des hommes'. The novel is therefore

74

contemporary and must present a 'real' picture of a society of which the reader is a part. The debate on what constitutes literary realism will rage through the nineteenth century and lies behind many of the controversies of our own age. Balzac, who was a man of the most wide-ranging curiosity, embracing science and philosophy as well as the arts, had a grandiose view of human society which he saw as a vast metaphorical translation of the world of nature. Just as there are natural species, he argued, so there are social species; as natural species evolve over thousands of generations as a result of their environment, so do social species develop. The differences between species like the lion, the reptile, insects and birds are no greater than the differences between human species like merchants, priests, soldiers, civil servants, although, in man, there are the added complications of intelligence, money and progress. The implications are clear: the novel is a serious form, it is concerned with contemporary affairs and with the social environment which shapes men and women for better or for worse. The genius of Balzac paints a world full of enormous creations, but it is a world in which all his characters are trapped. The death of Goriot is a scene of dramatic tragedy but it is the death of a man caught by a consuming passion for his daughters whose actions in turn are dictated by the corrupt values of a society to which they have totally surrendered. However magnificent Balzac's characters may be, they are not gifted with the power either to change or to transcend society.

The case of Flaubert is equally influential. If Balzac had striven to confer historical and philosophical status on the novel, Flaubert is concerned with the potential of the novel as an art-form and was the first to consider in any depth the aesthetic problems of fiction. His letters are full of the most penetrating observations; these, as in Balzac, are the product of his view of human nature. It is essentially pessimistic for he believes in a psychological determinism which rules the conduct of men and women. Victims of their own temperament and of their environment, they are doomed to live out lives from which they cannot escape. *Madame Bovary* (1857) is a great novel by any standard, an exploration in depth of a character so accurate and so universally true that it has given its name to a psychological state known as *bovarysme*, a form of self-deception which leads to a kind of paralysis of the will. Yet the characters are static. From our first meeting with Charles Bovary as a boy entering a classroom in a new school, clumsy, inarticulate, ridiculous with his monstrous hat, his life is set on a course of unintelligent, insensitive failure. Our first glimpse of Emma as a young woman emphasizes her sexuality; as a schoolgirl, she is shown to be lost in daydreams, pious, but concerned with the outward trappings of religiosity rather than with inner essences. The incompatibility between Charles and Emma is posed from the beginning; it grows and ends, as it must, in death and destruction. This is an essential part of Flaubert's belief in the presentation of human character in the novel; in a letter of February, 1867, discussing a contemporary novel, he makes clear how, in his view, the possibility of change or conversion in human character is so unlikely as to destroy the credibility of any novel which advances it:

> Je veux dire que les événements *ne dérivent plus* du caractère des personnages ou que ces mêmes caractères ne les produisent pas. Car c'est l'un ou l'autre (et même l'un et l'autre) dans la réalité. Les faits agissent sur nous et nous les causons. Ainsi, à quoi sert la révolution de Sicile? Déborah n'avait pas besoin de cela pour s'en aller, et Pipinna pour mourir. [These are references to events in the novel which Flaubert judged to be very unlikely.] Pourquoi ne pas leur avoir trouvé une fin en rapport naturel avec tous leurs antécédents? Cela est de la fantaisie et donne à une œuvre sérieusement commencée des apparences légères. Le roman, selon moi, doit être scientifique, c'est-à-dire rester dans les généralités probables.[1]

One can easily see in the novels of Zola the same dominance of environment and the same fatal development of the characters in a preordained path. The purpose of these remarks is to show that, in the novels of these three indisputably great novelists, there is a common factor: Balzac, Flaubert and Zola see their characters as imprisoned in a world, partially of their own making, from which they cannot escape. Their temperaments are such that they cannot transcend themselves and evolve in a new direction. Conversion from the self is denied to them. The technique employed to this end is imprecisely known as *realism*; given the importance of the environment, it leans heavily on physical description, using objects to give the reader insights into the characters. The uncut pages of the dusty medical encyclopaedia in Charles Bovary's surgery tell us more about his lack of medical curiosity than would pages of exposition. The twentieth century will challenge the vision of man powerless to alter his environment in society; its novelists will interpret 'reality' in a different way.

The seeds of dissent from these views are to be seen in Baudelaire and they reach full flower in the Symbolist movement at the end of the nineteenth century. Symbolism concentrates on meanings rather than on external appearances which are judged to be superficial; it is anti-materialist. The world of Zola's characters (an exact contemporary of the Symbolist movement) is a world in which there is no room for the arts, except as a manifestation of high neurosis but the Symbolists believe that art, although a purely *useless* activity in any material sense, is still the highest form of activity to which man can aspire. This powerful European movement posed a number of problems whose repercussions had a great influence on twentieth-century writers.

Firstly, there is a denial of the rôle of reality as it is displayed in the descriptive passages of the nineteenth-century novelists. At least some of their insistence on this method of 'situating' their characters was due to their desire to confer authenticity on the novel as a literary *genre* but Baudelaire's theory and practice of *correspondances* revealed an imaginative, visionary interpretation of life.[2] In the field of the novel, it is Proust who gives to reality a new meaning, more akin to Baudelaire than to Balzac. In the first pages of his novel *A la Recherche du temps perdu* (1913–27) occur these lines:

Un homme qui dort, tient en cercle autour de lui le fil des heures, l'ordre des années et des mondes.

In this statement Proust challenges traditional ways of representing the world. Reality, he argues, is not only, or even principally, what we can see and touch; it is this, but more than this. The impact of the world upon us is recorded by all our senses and when we recall the experiences, they are indissolubly linked with all the circumstances of the time: the state of our mind, of our body, the events of our life. This impact can be preserved intact by the memory and its total recall abolishes the traditional compartmentalization of time into past, present and future. There are many ideas here which will exercise twentieth-century writers: what is reality and how can it be represented? What is the mechanism of the human mind? What is time?

Secondly, Symbolism denies the materialistic view of man as prisoner of his social environment. In many cases, this takes the form of the creation of cerebral characters who try to deny the world by ignoring it, like Remy de Gourmont's *Sixtine* (1890) which was heavily influenced by J.-K. Huysman's *A Rebours* (1884), the very textbook of this escape from life. The hero, Des Esseintes, deliberately turns his back on existence to live in an artificial, enclosed world. The final collapse of his illusions leaves him groping for religion in a curiously prophetic forecast of Huysman's own life. In a preface to a new edition of *A Rebours* published some twenty years on, Huysmans concluded a critique of the book and a gloss of his state of mind at the time by saying that the author, at the end of his novel, had only two alternatives, the revolver or the foot of the Cross. Huysmans chose Catholicism, one of a number of writers whose return to the faith signified a revival of Christianity as a force among writers. The symbolist ethic is concerned more with the rejection of life than with reform and revolution. As such, it has little success in the twentieth century but its denial of the idea that man is trapped by a hostile environment restores freedom to him and encourages reformulations of the

77

rôle of man in society. André Gide, who was strongly influenced by the symbolist movement as a young man, is a very significant figure in this debate.

In his novel, *Les Faux-Monnayeurs* (1926), Gide, through the character of Edouard—himself a novelist—reflects on the nineteenth-century novel and rejects Balzac's method's of conferring authentic life on his characters, to give them an 'état civil' as he describes it. More generally, Gide absolutely rejects deterministic explanations of man, which deny him the freedom of choice; here he is a powerful influence on those writers who were born at the turn of the century. It is not that Gide deliberately sought disciples; indeed, in a note prefacing *Les Nourritures terrestres* (1897), he wrote:

> Et quand tu m'auras lu, jette ce livre—et sors. Je voudrais qu'il t'eût donné le désir de sortir—sortir de n'importe où, de ta chambre, de ta pensée, de ta ville, de ta famille. N'emporte pas mon livre avec toi.

This may be a denial of leadership but the tremendous call to liberty was eagerly heard. The Gidean figure is sheltered from economic reality which plays little part in the fictional works. The conflicts of these middle-class characters are moral, religious and domestic. They are at war with convention and with each other, in search of self-gratification and hedonism. The effect of the novels is very far from being doctrinaire, for in a preface to the second edition of *Paludes* (1895), Gide wrote:

> J'aime que chaque livre porte en lui, mais cachée, sa propre réfutation et ne s'assoie pas sur l'idée, de peur qu'on n'en voie l'autre face. J'aime qu'il porte en lui de quoi se nier, se supprimer lui-même.[3]

So, in *La Porte étroite* (1909), for example, the reader is invited to consider the case of Alissa who breaks off her engagement to Jérôme. What are her motives? Are they purely religious and mystical in their origin? Or are they caused by sexual frigidity, rationalized into a religious argument? Are they a revolt against her mother's very different conduct? Are they the obscure assertion of the more dominating Alissa against the ineffectual Jérôme? Are they the well disguised symptoms of the traditional female attitude of playing hard to get, carried to extremes? All these questions may be asked and a plausible answer can be given to each. Human attitudes are seen as complicated, inexplicable, unpredictable and, above all, *free*. It is difficult to envisage any nineteenth-century novelist writing a work of this kind. To this climate of moral ambiguity, which is in itself, a release, one must add the Gidean concept of 'l'acte gratuit'. Much has been written on this but here is how Gide himself explains it:

> Mais non, je ne crois pas, pas du tout, à un acte gratuit. Même je tiens celui-ci pour parfaitement impossible à concevoir, à imaginer. Il y toujours une motivation à

toute chose; mais j'entends par 'acte gratuit' un acte dont la motivation n'est pas apparente, et qui présente les caractères du désintéressement. Un acte qui n'est pas accompli en vue de tel profit ou récompense, mais qui répond à une impulsion secrète, dans lequel ce que l'individu a de plus particulier se révèle, se trahit.[4]

To think of the 'acte gratuit' as being without motive is wrong for its motivation is to be found deep in the mind and personality. By the commonly accepted rules of social convention, it may seem to be gratuitous but in fact it may be altruistic, or even a rebellious act by which man expresses himself. It is now clear how important the rehabilitation of the individual in Gide is a liberating force for his successors.

If a man is condemned to be free, as J.-P. Sartre will say, what guidelines will he follow? The religious revival which began at the end of the nineteenth century found its protagonists in a number of writers who interpreted the world in a Christian sense and argued with authority that this is the only meaning which makes sense. Playwrights like Claudel, poets and critics like Péguy, novelists like Bernanos and François Mauriac, philosophers like Maritain, Gabriel Marcel, Simone Weil and Teilhard de Chardin were not so much Catholic propagandists as writers whose exegesis of the world was Christian. As François Mauriac said, men are given 'le pouvoir de dire non à la loi qui les écrase'. This is how, by God's help, the Catholic writer sees man imposing his will on society and working for its betterment. But if you are not a Christian, on what can you base a moral code which will apply both to individuals and society? We have seen that Camus believes the world to be absurd. In the absence of God, it is the duty of man to join in collective revolt, to work with love and compassion against cruelty and injustice. The existentialist ethic, whilst not accepting solidarity to this extent, puts the responsibility on the individual himself. There is, of course, a third possibility. The growth of communism as a political force appeared to present a moral, ethical, economic and political answer to the problems of the century but the excesses of intolerance practised in its name alienated many intellectuals; the figure of Tarrou in *La Peste* is a case in point.

The moral *disponibilité* of man soon ceased to be a matter for theoretical debate as a result of the drastic impact of world events. The 1914–18 war had a shattering impact for it caused the death or wounding of about fourteen million young men. The survivors, after being given temporary hope by the founding of the League of Nations, soon lapsed into despair as nations returned to traditional attitudes, with the same politicians mouthing the same platitudes. Words like 'liberty' and 'justice' became empty catchwords justifying the worst excesses. André Breton, one of the leaders of the Surrealists, put it well:

> Je dis que ce que l'attitude surréaliste, au départ, a eu de commun avec celle de Lautréamont et Rimbaud et ce qui, une fois pour toutes, a enchaîné notre sort au leur, c'est le DEFAITISME de guerre [. . .] A nos yeux, le champ n'était libre que pour une révolution étendue vraiment à tous les domaines, invraisemblablement radicale, extrêmement répressive [5]

The Thirties proved to be a testing time for these attitudes. The growth of totalitarian régimes in Germany and Italy under Hitler and Mussolini brought a peculiarly hateful form of government, based on a false idea of racial supremacy, on systematic persecution ardent in its attacks on individual freedom. A key work of this period is André Malraux's *La Condition humaine* (1933) which was a powerful influence on both Sartre and Camus. Malraux here defined, sharply and dramatically, the problem of modern man in society: his solitude, his anguish, the violence of political systems against the individual, the suffering and dignity of man, his feeling of alienation mingled with a sense of fraternity with other men. The bombing of Guernica in 1937 during the Spanish Civil War was an act of peculiar horror for it was an open, undefended town in which the many victims were the old, women and children. It inspired in Picasso the angry masterpiece entitled 'Guernica'. The persecution of the Jews by the Nazis was a most direct affront to human life and dignity. So, gradually, the concept of war, which, after 1918, had seemed to be hideous and indefensible, was gradually revised to include the concept of a 'just' war. The Second World War (1939–45) became inevitable and its five years of Occupation by Germany complicated the issues until they became more than a straightforward battle between Fascism and Democracy. Problems of compromise in government were much to the fore (see Anouilh's *Antigone* of 1944). The issues of Marxism were hotly debated; its theories of social justice and equality were obviously tempting to those who fought for the freedom and dignity of the individual. Its practical applications in post-war Europe often appeared less tempting and *Les Mains sales* is only one of many works in which this is debated.

What appears increasingly clear in the twentieth century is that the chaos of violence is to be laid at the door of man himself; there is no alibi available to him. A general movement in the fields of philosophy, psychology, medicine and literature had begun to study in depth the mysteries of the human mind and subconscious. The debate on reason versus the imagination which we have seen in Baudelaire is continued but in a context wider than that of literature. If the pursuit of reason has led to the disastrous events of the twentieth century, is it not time that man should trust to the imagination? Should we not seek to know ourselves more profoundly? Guillaume Apollinaire, in his poem *La Jolie Rousse*, hints at the excitements which these new searches can discover, when he speaks on behalf of his fellow-writers:

> Nous ne sommes pas vos ennemis
> Nous voulons vous donner de vastes et d'étranges domaines
> Où le mystère en fleurs s'offre à qui veut le cueillir
> Il y a là des feux nouveaux des couleurs jamais vues
> Mille phantasmes impondérables
> Auxquels il faut donner de la réalité
> Nous voulons explorer la bonté contrée énorme où tout se tait
> Il y a aussi le temps qu'on peut chasser ou faire revenir
> Pitié pour nous qui combattons toujours aux frontières
> De l'illimité et de l'avenir.[6]

The writings of Sigmund Freud (1856–1939) on the analysis of the subconscious were widely translated and much read in France. Here indeed was to be found a direct challenge to established ideas on reality, on logic, on the limits of the human mind. If we had previously thought of reality as a set of concepts perceived by the conscious mind, what status can we give to what is perceived in the subconscious? If we experience a dream or a nightmare as 'real', is it no more than a fantasy, or is it a true illumination? André Breton, one of the leaders of Surrealism with Louis Aragon and Paul Eluard, was a medical student who became passionately interested in Freudian psychoanalysis. Now it seemed that the imagination was authenticated, that dream and hallucination became reliable modes of understanding. During the height of the surrealist movement in the twenties and thirties, the exploration of the unconscious is seen as the most urgent preoccupation of writers and artists. Here, perhaps, lay the dimension that Surrealism sought in André Breton's definition:

> Tout porte à croire qu'il existe un certain point de l'esprit d'où la vie et la mort, le réel et l'imaginaire, le passé et le futur, le communicable et l'incommunicable, le haut et le bas cessent d'être perçus contradictoirement. C'est en vain qu'on cherecherait à l'activité surréaliste un autre mobile que l'espoir de détermination de ce point.[7]

In attempting to resolve the most absolute contradictions that we have for centuries become educated to see as totally incompatible, such as life and death, the real and the imaginary, Breton demonstrates the surrealist attack on reason. It is a continuation of ideas first launched by the short-lived anarchistic movement called Dada which had descended on Paris at the end of the 1914–18 war. The implications of these radical views can be explained: the Surrealists argue that the way we perceive the world is largely a habit since our perceptions have become codified by traditional ways of thinking, masquerading as reason, bolstered by accepted moral, political and social beliefs. The subsconscious appears to be a great untapped source of knowledge of man. Baudelaire's views on the imagination are refined and it becomes firmly enthroned as the prime agent of discovery, as, for example, in Eugène Ionesco's statement made in 1960:

> La liberté d'imagination n'est pas une fuite dans l'irréel, elle n'est pas une évasion, elle est audace, invention. Inventer n'est pas démissionner, n'est pas s'évader. Les routes de l'imagination sont innombrables, les puissances de l'invention n'ont pas de bornes.[8]

What is being demanded is a new habit of seeing and thinking. From its earliest days the twentieth century has seen a ferment of experiment in all the arts which has, all too often, degenerated into a frenzied search for originality at any price. The interrelationship of the arts has seen reciprocal influences, particularly between literature and painting. Above all, traditional techniques have been questioned and often rejected in favour of the 'modern' and the avant-garde. The modern is, of course, in a constant state of change; as it becomes itself another way of conforming, it seeks other directions but it is possible to distinguish certain characteristics which particularly belong to the age.

Firstly, there is the preoccupation with language. Mallarmé, in his sonnet, *Le Tombeau d'Edgar Poe*, had proclaimed his ambition to

> Donner un sens plus pur aux mots de la tribu

and this disquiet at what was seen as the 'impurity' of language was also felt by Paul Valéry. Valéry's solution is to seek complete precision in the use of language; obsessed by his desire for *rigueur* in thought, Valéry struggled to attain a language which represented the exact measure, no more and no less, of his thought. More radical is the statement of Guillaume Apollinaire:

> O bouches l'homme est à la recherche d'un nouveau langage
> Auquel le grammairien d'aucune langue n'aura rien à dire
>
> Et ces vieilles langues sont tellement près de mourir
> Que c'est vraiment par habitude et manque d'audace
> Qu'on les fait encore servir à la poésie.[9]

The theme of renewal in language is at the heart of surrealist doctrine, although here certain excesses led to a difficulty in communication which ended in considerable obscurity. After all, lucidity is still an essential quality in literature. Paul Eluard, a surrealist leader, expressed plainly the distrust of rhetoric:

> Rien de plus affreux que le langage poétisé, que des mots trop jolis gracieusement liés à d'autres perles. La poésie véritable s'accommode de nudités crues, de planches qui ne sont pas de salut, de larmes qui ne sont pas irisées. Elle sait qu'il y a des

déserts de boue, des parquets cirés, des chevelures decoiffées, des mains rugueuses, des victimes puantes, des héros misérables, des idiots superbes, toutes les sortes de chiens, des balais, des fleurs dans l'herbe, des fleurs sur les tombes. Car la poésie est dans la vie.[10]

The preoccupation with language is fundamental, for what one can say depends on the kind of language one is able to use. Style is part of the way one sees the world as Ionesco clearly saw:

Renouveler le langage c'est renouveler la conception, la vision du monde.[11]

These two statements go to the heart of the matter. Language has become a series of clichés and hinders communication between men; if we are to re-establish communication, the layered accretions of language must be cleared. Ionesco's play, *La Cantatrice chauve* (1950), is one of the clearest demonstrations of the opaque nature of language where slogan replaces thought and people cannot talk because they no longer think or question their actions. So it is that poets of the twentieth century follow the lead of Rimbaud and abolish discriminations between what had for centuries been thought of as 'poetic' and 'unpoetic' words, that is, words which were suitable for use in poetry and those which were not. Apollinaire employs a technique of shock to surprise the reader by unexpected words and images. When he writes:

Bergère ô tour Eiffel le troupeau des ponts bêle ce matin

he is combining, in a totally unexpected way, the traditional pastoral image of shepherdess and sheep with a scene from contemporary life. The shock contained in:

Les becs de gaz pissaient leur flamme au clair de lune

is much more obvious and superficial but in these lines, from *La Chanson du mal-aimé*, a poem full of the grief and hate of disappointed love, the result is more complicated:

Et moi, j'ai le coeur aussi gros
Qu'un cul de dame damascène.

Coming after verses where the poet's chagrin is described in terms of tragic deception, the reader expects the comparison 'aussi gros que' to lead to some immense statement but the actual object to which his grief is compared is vulgarly—and comically—deflating. It is thus that the use of language is challenged. The Surrealists tried more drastic methods of the renewal of language by the practice of *l'écriture automatique*. André Breton described the method of automatic writing in his *Manifeste du surréalisme*:

Faites-vous apporter de quoi écrire, après vous être établi en un lieu aussi favorable que possible à la concentration de votre esprit sur lui-même. Placez-vous dans l'état le plus passif, ou réceptif que vous pourrez. Faites abstraction de votre génie, de vos talents et de ceux de tous les autres. Dites-vous bien que la littérature est un des plus tristes chemins qui mènent à tout. Ecrivez vite sans sujet préconçu, aussi vite pour ne pas retenir et ne pas être tenté de vous relire.[12]

This procedure is not reserved only for poets but is available to all. It denies lucidity which is the enemy of revelation and sets great store on speed, rather than on revision. One writes at the dictation of the subconscious, explicit meaning is not the aim.

The practice of automatic writing is only one of the ways in which traditional forms of literature were undermined. It is in literature that language is enshrined and the revitalization of language necessarily involves a break with literary forms. The complex and rigorous systems of prosody which had been elaborated in France over centuries were overthrown. Free verse, first used by certain symbolist poets at the end of the nineteenth century, knew a great popularity; punctuation largely disappeared from poetry and all prohibitions of vocabulary were removed. Typography was called in to reinforce verbal effects as in Apollinaire's *Calligrammes* (1918). The attitude of Anti-Art adopted by writers of the avant-garde fathered the Anti-novel and the Anti-theatre. Ionesco has confessed how shocked he was to hear the audience laugh at performances of *La Cantatrice chauve* for he had considered it to be 'a tragic spectacle of human life reduced to passionless automatism through bourgeois convention and the fossilization of language'.[13] He has warned his audiences by the blurring of opposites in his subtitles to plays: 'anti-pièces', 'drames comiques', 'pseudo-drames' and 'farces tragiques'. Traditional literary forms assume a continuation of standards and ideas which are no longer in existence.

One of the most powerful weapons of the avant-garde, in which experiment, attack and destruction are combined, is to be found in the use of laughter. The powerful possibilities of satire and the destructive rôle of the comic form a significant part of the French literary tradition from Rabelais, through Molière and Voltaire to Alfred Jarry (1873–1907, one of the saints in the calendar of the Absurd). Apollinaire saw this unerringly in his famous lecture on *L'Esprit nouveau et les poètes* in 1917,[14] in which he said:

Nous avons vu aussi depuis Alfred Jarry le rire s'élever des basses régions où il se tordait et fournir au poète un lyrisme tout neuf. Où est le temps où le mouchoir de Desdémone paraissait d'un ridicule inadmissible? Aujourd'hui, le ridicule même est poursuivi, on cherche à s'en emparer et il a sa place dans la poésie, parce qu'il fait partie de la vie au même titre que l'héroïsme et tout ce qui nourrissait jadis l'enthousiasme des poètes.

It is clear that Apollinaire insists upon the creative power of laughter to liberate the spirit and so to shatter preconceived ideas. In the theatre this led to 'the dethronement of language and logic' as Martin Esslin has called it and provides a new experience in theatrical terms. For other avant-garde writers it provided a spur towards a lyricism of discontinuity in which humour—*l'humour noir*—plays a large part. Surrealist artists exploited it by the creation of objects in which the unexpected and irrational juxtaposition of perfectly ordinary objects and materials created a new and disquieting thing. Such are the *Cadeau* of Man Ray, a flat-iron with a row of tintacks placed, point outwards, on its flat base, or the cup, saucer and spoon made of fur by Meret Oppenheim. These objects are amusing, but it is the laughter of disquiet and embarrassment. What do they mean? Of what use can they be? It is one more attack on reason.

Although the avant-garde has attracted to itself an enormous amount of publicity, it is not the only manifestation of the questing human spirit of the twentieth century. Malraux, Sartre and Camus all saw the absurdity of the world. Their collective definition of this state embraces the recognition of its violence, cruelty and injustice; the anguish and isolation of men were expressed in moral, political and even metaphysical terms. In their novels and plays they acted out the implications of alienation and tentatively advanced methods for solution and reasons for hope: the solidarity of men, the meaning and justification of revolt, human dignity, the responsibilities of existentialist man. Now these three writers are not described as writers of the avant-garde and the novel, demanding as it does the solution to long and arduous problems of composition, is not a genre in which the avant-garde was particularly involved. Nevertheless, their novels represent a radically new approach to the analysis of the human condition; novels like *La Condition humaine* (1933), *La Nausée* (1938) and *La Peste* (1947) must surely claim a place in any list of the great novels of the age. Malraux, Sartre and Camus are literary technicians of high skill but they are not innovators in form and so avoid the self-created difficulties into which a number of their contemporaries fell. This is perhaps the principal crisis of 'modernism'.

The attack on the traditional forms and styles of literature stemmed in part from the belief that these are ineradicably linked to traditional ways of thinking and to a system of ideas which the avant-garde wish to break. In addition, there is the belief that, as in the Symbolist movement, literature had become increasingly the perquisite of an élite, with writers deliberately addressing themselves to the small group of initiates. If literature is to become an instrument of change it must be made available to all readers.

Many of the verbal techniques of the avant-garde led to an increasing obscurity which alienated the very public they were seeking to attract. This is the dilemma that was noted by Camus:

> L'erreur de l'art moderne est presque toujours de faire passer le moyen avant la fin, la forme avant le fond, la technique avant le sujet. Si les techniques d'art me passionnent et si je cherche à les posséder toutes c'est que je veux pouvoir m'en servir librement, les réduire au rang d'outils.[15]

The same point has been made more sharply in an introduction to his collected articles on jazz by Philip Larkin, himself nevertheless a significant but discreet innovator:

> [. . .] the term 'modern', when applied to art, has a more than chronological meaning: it denotes a quality of irresponsibility peculiar to this century, known sometimes as modernism, and once I had classified modern jazz under this heading I knew where I was. I am sure there are books in which the genesis of modernism is set out in full. My own theory is that it is related to an imbalance between the two tensions from which art springs: these are the tension between the artist and his material, and between the artist and his audience, and that in the last 75 years or so the second of these has slackened or even perished. In consequence the artist has become over-concerned with his material (hence an age of technical experiment), and, in isolation, has busied himself with the two principal themes of modernism, mystification and outrage.[16]

It is not possible even to attempt a conclusion. The search for hope, meaning and identity continues, the avant-garde renews itself. New happenings raise new questions, new writers suggest new enlightenments. Time brings a different perspective and reminds us that what is 'relevant' to our knowledge of the human condition is by no means limited to the contemporary. I sometimes think that one of the greatest gifts a teacher can give to a pupil is a sense of wonder at the potential of man—for good as well as evil.

NOTES

1 *Correspondance*, nouvelle édition augmentée, Paris, Conard, 1929, vol.V, p.277.
2 For a discussion on this point, see earlier, 'The Poetry of Baudelaire'.
3 *Romans, Récits et Soties, Œuvres lyriques*, Paris, Pléiade, 1958, p.1,479.
4 *Ibid.*, p.1,571.
5 In *Qu'est-ce que le surréalisme?*, Brussels, Henriquez, 1934.
6 *Calligrammes*, 1918.
7 *Dictionnaire abrégé du surréalisme*, 1938.
8 *Notes et contrenotes*, Paris, Gallimard, 1962, p.64.
9 'La Victoire' in *Calligrames*.
10 'Les Sentiers et les routes de la poésie', *Oeuvres complètes*, Paris, Pléiade, vol.II, pp.530–1.
11 *Op. cit.*, p.85.
12 For a discussion on this subject, see A. Alexandrian, *André Breton par lui-même*, Paris, Ed.du Seuil, 1971, pp.37 *foll.*
13 Martin Esslin, *The Theatre of the Absurd*, revised ed., London, Pelican Books, 1968, p.138.
14 *Oeuvres complètes de Guillaume Apollinaire*, ed. M. Décaudin, Paris, Balland & Lecat, vol.3 1966, p.905.
15 'Dernier interview d'Albert Camus, 20 décembre 1959', *Essais*, Paris, Pléiade, 1967, p.19,27.
16 *All What Jazz, a Record Diary 1961–68*, London, Faber & Faber 1970, p.11.